"**Sustaining The Vision Workbook**" is designed to equip the vision carrier with understanding their destiny and calling and writing their vision, while acquiring Godly revelation on how to pray, release, plow, and sustain in the destiny and calling of God on his or her life. It will assist the vision carrier in learning how to govern the vision as a pure visionary, and how to lead in excellence and SHIFT those who are called to help bring the vision to pass. This book is sure to SHIFT the vision carrier into towering in who they are in God and successfully achieving the calling, destiny, and vision that God has granted to the vision carrier's hands.

SUSTAINING THE VISION WORKBOOK

TaquettaBaker@Kingdomshifters.com

(Website) Kingdomshifters.com

Connect with Taquetta via Facebook or YouTube

Copyright 2018 – Kingdom Shifters Ministries

All rights reserved. This book is protected by the copyright laws of the United States of America. This book may not be reprinted for commercial gain or profit. The use of occasional page copying for personal or group study is permitted and encouraged. Permission will be granted upon request.

Taquetta's Bio

Taquetta Baker is the founder of Kingdom Shifters Ministries (KSM). She has authored fourteen books and two decree CD's. Taquetta has a Master's Degree in Community Counseling with an emphasis on Marriage, Children and Family Counseling, a Bachelor's Degree in Psychology and Associates Degree in Business Administration. In addition, Taquetta has a Therapon Belief Therapist Certification from Therapon Institute and has 22 years of professional and Christian Counseling experience.

Taquetta is also gifted at empowering and assisting people with launching ministries, businesses and books and provides mentoring, counseling and vision casting through Kingdom Shifters Kingdom Wellness Program. Taquetta serves on the Board of Directors for New Day Community Ministries, Inc. of Muncie, IN. In October 2008, Taquetta graduated from the Eagles Dance Institute under Dr. Pamela Hardy and received her license in the area of liturgical dance. Before launching into her own ministry, Taquetta served at her previous church for 12 years. She was a prophet, pioneer and leader of Shekinah Expressions Dance Ministry, teacher, member of the presbytery board, and overseer of the Altar Workers Ministry. Taquetta receives mentoring and ministry covering from Bishop Jackie Green, Founder of JGM-National PrayerLife Institute (Phoenix, AZ), and was ordained as an Apostle on June 7, 2014.

Taquetta flows through the wells of warfare and worship and mantles an apostolic mandate of judging and establishing God's kingdom in people, ministries, communities, and regions. Taquetta travels in foreign missions and throughout the United States. She has mentored and established dance, altar workers, deliverance, and prophetic ministries. Taquetta ministers in the areas of fine arts, all manners of prayer, fivefold ministry, deliverance, healing, miracles, atmospheric worship, and empowers and train people in their destiny and life's vision.

Connect with Taquetta and KSM at kingdomshifters.com or via Facebook. For more information regarding Bishop Jackie Green at Jgmenternational.org.

Table Of Contents

SEEKING GOD FOR THE VISION 1
BUILDING A DESTINY RELATIONSHIP WITH GOD 4
BIBLICAL ENGRAVEMENTS OF VISION PLANS 7
WISDOM KEYS FOR ACCOUNTABILITY TO VISION PLANS 13
KNOWING YOUR DESTINY VISION 15
HOW TO WRITE A PERSONAL DESTINY PLAN 27
WRITING YOUR PERSONAL DESTINY VISION PLAN 32
GOD DESIRES US TO PROSPER 35
MONEY! MONEY! MONEY! MONEY! 39
WRITING YOUR ENTREPRENEURIAL VISION PLAN! 45
SHORT & LONG-TERM VISION PLAN 51
CHARACTER OF AN ENTREPRENEURIAL VISION CARRIER 54
NUGGETS FOR LAUNCHING MARKETPLACE ENDEAVORS 57
NUGGETS FOR SOCIAL MEDIA ADVERTISING 64
DESPISE NOT SMALL BEGINNINGS 66
DECLARATION OF INDEPENDENCE 68
OBEDIENCE TO THE VISION 75
YOUR ACCOUNTABILITY TRIBE 82
THE REGION KNOWS YOUR NAME 88
DELIVERANCE FROM SELF-SABATOGE 99
CONQUERING DESTINY KILLING SPIRITS 105
WARFARE STRATEGIES 111
SPIRITUAL CLEANSING! MAINTAINING DELIVERANCE! 119
BALANCING LIFE, DESTINY & THE VISION 132
SUGGESTIONS FOR TAKING RESPITE 138
BALANCING FAMILY & RELATIONSHIPS 142
ESTABLISHING SUCCESSORS 146
YEAR END REFLECTION & NEW YEAR GOALS 150
VISIONARY CHARGE! SHIFT 159

FOREWORD

At a time like this when there is such an increase of those beginning to shift into an entrepreneurial mindset, this workbook is a crucial necessity! Although this mindset shift is great and can lead to individual freedom from the 9am to 5pm job, it can also be dangerous and detrimental if not began correctly and given the right foundation to stand upon through the process. It is one thing to begin an entrepreneurial vision that does not have its roots in God, but it is a whole other to begin a vision that God has ordained for your life that will lead to the fulfillment of your destiny and calling.

When Steve Jobs created Apple and Mark Zuckerberg created Facebook, their focus was on their vision, success, and wealth alone, not the glory of another. From much of what we have heard about concerning the internal affairs of their companies and its development, it involved a lot of backstabbing, dishonor, fame and glory seeking, lack of integrity, loss friendships and torn relationships, and the list can go on and on. However, these types of occurrences cannot and should not be a part of a God ordained vision. There is more weight, responsibility, and accountability that comes with the establishing and sustaining of a godly entrepreneurial vision. It requires godly character, nature, honor, humility, integrity, wisdom, strong prayer foundation, divine connections, godly relationships and etc. In God, no matter what your vision, service, or product provides, it is for his glory, to make his name known greater in the earth, and to advance his kingdom. Therefore, we cannot go about our vision just any old way. There is a blueprint. There is a plan. There is a path that God has preordained for your vision's success. We must become aware of it, access it, and shift into it!

This workbook will help you do just that. It walks you from A-Z concerning beginning, sustaining, and fulfilling your vision. The questions asked may take you some time to think through, but as you spend time hearing from the Lord for the answers, the clarity, definition, and strong foundation needed will be cultivated during this time. In partaking of the revelation of this workbook and walking through the steps provided, you will ensure that you understand the entirety of your vision beyond just today and have prepared it to flourish from generation to generation. You will also be able to implement these practices into the upkeep of your vision and cultivate them as a part of your destiny lifestyle. This workbook is so important and it is great that those who receive it will not only walk in their vision, but will have foresight on things to expect with strategy on how to overcome. May this workbook be life changing for you and be a significant stepping stone as you dive into greater depths in establishing and succeeding in your God ordained entrepreneurial vision. Decreeing that the fruit will be evident and a blessing to you and all who partake of the vision that God has granted to your hands!

Written by Minister Nina Cook, Apostle Taquetta's Spiritual Daughter and Armorbearer

FOREWORD

Entrepreneurs are a vital piece to the world today. Entrepreneurs help guide the economy, create wealth streams, impact their communities and spheres of influence in so many wonderful ways, and they are vision carriers that have the ability to impact change for generations after. Being an Entrepreneur is a great honor, but it does come with a weight. In order to be able to sustain and navigate through an ever changing economy and a competitive advantage it is a monumental necessity that our mindset of being and entrepreneur shift to a kingdom mindset, where we are seated in heavenly places and can see the bigger picture to gain greater strategy. Entrepreneurship is not just about a good idea, but it is about your identity, destiny, and calling, and what God has required of you to release in the earth.

This workbook equips you with an array of strategies and tools to not only help write the vision and make it plan, but to search inward and see if there is anything that would hinder the vision from being able to grow, maintain, and sustain through each season. As the vision carriers, it is important to search ourselves and receive the healing and deliverance we need in order to build the vison on a solid foundation that is fortified in Jesus Christ.

This workbook is strategically set up in a way that provokes you to think beyond the surface and shift you into a deeper cultivating relationship with God. If you are honest and open, as you write and spend time with the Lord concerning every question and activation, the vison will become clear and you will have a firm stance that will not easily be swayed, and no matter what service or product you provide you will know that it is developed and operating in the excellency of God and he pleased.

Decreeing the fruit of the true entrepreneur and visionary is arising and SHIFTING you as you partake and activate!

Minister Amanda Barnhill, Emerging Entrepreneur, Apostle Taquetta's Administrator and Mentee

SEEKING GOD FOR THE VISION

Often, we will have a dream, vision, word, desire, or unction from God to write a book, start a business, organization or ministry, but we will not know how to go about starting it.

> ***Habakkuk 2:1-4*** *I will stand upon my watch, and set me upon the tower, and will watch to see what he will say unto me, and what I shall answer when I am reproved. And the Lord answered me, and said, Write the vision, and make it plain upon tables, that he may run that readeth it.*
>
> *For the vision is yet for an appointed time, but at the end it shall speak, and not lie: though it tarry, wait for it; because it will surely come, it will not tarry. Behold, his soul which is lifted up is not upright in him: but the just shall live by his faith.*

Habakkuk took a stand and established himself upon the tower, so he could watch for what God was saying and desiring for him, the call of God for his life, and those he was leading.

A tower is a high place, a mound, fortress, siege, entrenchment, and enclosure.

It is generally upon a horizon which yields what is to come - or yield the beginnings and future of things. It reveals that which is afar off.

Because the tower is upon the horizon, it also allows the watchman
- ✓ To see who is coming and going
- ✓ See the enemy afar off
- ✓ Provides the watchman time to signal and warn that the enemy is approaching or what is occurring in the distance

Habakkuk SHIFTED himself to a heightened dimension in God, while enclosing himself in this realm where he could see past his circumstances into the truth and will of God. This was a time of consecration for he took a time of stillness before the Lord, "I will stand upon my watch, and set me upon the tower, and will watch to see what he will say."

Sometimes we must put all else aside and spend time seeking God regarding the specific plans for the vision, desires, and dreams he has given us. If we are not hearing him, it is probably because we are too engulfed in the things and cares of life. SHIFT to a consecrated place where you can see, hear, and receive the vision of the Lord.

- God may show you the beginning and the ending, while encouraging you to walk with him in faith with planting and filling the vision with his word.
- God may give you bits and pieces of the plan and as you implement that, he will unfold more.

- God may tell you that the plan has a specific appointed time of coming to pass, and may begin to do things in you and through you to prepare you to be a vision carrier.

Prayer Assignment:
> - Spend time hearing God for your destiny and life's vision. Soak yourself in the truth of what he reveals to you.
> - Be okay if he does not speak right away and commit to a seven, fourteen, or twenty-one-day consecration, to commune and explore your life's vision with the Lord.
> - During this time of consecration, practice building a lifetime relationship with God, where you can walk with him when he is speaking and when he is silent. This is important because destiny is not necessarily a destination or a goal you are trying to reach, as those points of success are just destiny moments. Destiny however, is a lifestyle of living in the will, plan, and purposes God ordained for you at birth. Destiny is not just a moment with God, but a journey in and with God. Destiny is a lifestyle. You will need constant communing and knowing the heart, spirit, character and nature of God to achieve destiny.

As you seek God from this new horizon, journal your consecration experience.

BUILDING A DESTINY RELATIONSHIP WITH GOD

Want to know what God desires of you? Simply ask him. God enjoys communing with his people. If he does not speak right away, do not take that as rejection. Sometimes God wants us to want more than just answers so spend time with him even in silence. God desires us to build a lasting relationship with him, where such communion becomes our lifestyle.

1. **Communication** - communicating your thoughts, feelings, desires to God and allowing him to do the same. Being open to constructive criticism and to changing for the better of self and the relationship.

2. **Honesty** - being honest in your communication. Even being honest about your fears, hurts, pains, joys, what you do not agree with, what you need clarity for or patience with, etc. If God urgently needs something from you, he will equip you or reveal to you how you are already equip. Otherwise, you will find him to be a patient God that is willing to journey in the process with you. You must be honest, so his grace can prevail where your pride and insecurity surrender you to leaning on and trusting him.

3. **Vulnerability** - Please know that communication = vulnerability. There is no way to communicate effectively without being vulnerable. Striving to protect ourselves from being rejected, hurt, and disappointed causes more agony and consequences than being vulnerable. I say this because we risk losing or never obtaining the very thing we say we want. We fail to give ourselves a voice and opportunity to have our needs and desires met. ***Psalms 138:8*** *The LORD will perfect that which concerneth me: thy mercy, O LORD, endureth for ever: forsake not the works of thine own hands*

4. **Trust** - When God says he will never leave or forsake you, he means it. You can take God at his word. It never returns void. The key is being in alignment to connect with his word as it comes to pass. And even when you miss it, God will provide opportunities for you to connect with his word again. He wants you to receive what he has for you. Trust shifts us to a place where obedience is not a chore but a desire and choice to have confidence in the will of God for our lives and for what we say we desire out of life. ***Deuteronomy 31:6*** *Be strong and of a good courage, fear not, nor be afraid of them: for the LORD thy God, he it is that doth go with thee; he will not fail thee, nor forsake thee.*

5. **Respect** - Respect demonstrates a conscious honor, reverence, gratitude and consideration for another. We tend to respect people based on their positions, abilities, beliefs, etc., but God requires us to also respect one another simply because we exist together. God requires us to respect him and his position as our God, and to honor and respect him by keeping his commandments. ***1John 2:5*** *But if anyone obeys his word, love for God is truly made complete in them. This is how we know we are in him.*

6. **Patience** - Just like you need God to be patient with you, you must be patient with God. Often, we perceive patience as not getting what we want when we want it. Patience is a fruit of the spirit and a fruit starts out as a seed that grows into a fruit. Patience is the ability to grow into something with someone or grow towards a goal or desire. It requires cultivation to watch a seed blossom into what it is going to be. This is where you are able to further work your relationship with God and even with that which you are waiting on. You are able to go deeper in communion where you walk with him in the uncomfortable times, times of expectation, and times of uncertainty, while that which you are waiting on flourishes into that which you receive or achieve.

7. **Quality Time** - Is time spent in giving another one's undivided attention in order to strengthen a relationship. Quality time can be simply resting in the presence of God as it can be communicative or no communication. We always want God to be talking but this is a relationship of performance rather than a balanced relationship where every facet of the relationship is developed, cultivated, and prospering. *Revelations 3:20 Behold, I stand at the door, and knock: if any man hear my voice, and open the door, I will come in to him, and will sup with him, and he with me.*

8. **Agreement & Covenant Cooperation** – Our entire relationship with God is about restoring and resting in the covenant that was originally ours before the fall of Adam and Eve. We must come into agreement with that covenant and allow God to lead us into the truth, grace, wellness, protection, and prosperity that is rightfully ours. Our agreement must be verbal. It also must manifest through our daily actions and submitted posture to who God has created us to be in the earth.

9. **Individuality Appreciation** - Often we are challenged by God's uniqueness because we do not understand it. When we think we have a grasp on who he is, he unveils another level of himself. This should not intimidate or frustrate us as if we really consider ourselves - if we are truly walking in alignment and relationship with the Lord, we too are always evolving and changing. The deliverance, healing, and building ourselves in the character and nature of God should be continuously transforming us into the standard of God. We have to appreciate how he evolves and reveals himself to us, how we evolve and reveal ourselves to the world, and how others evolve and reveal themselves to us and the world.

10. **Praise & Worship Empowerment** - Praise and worship opens a portal that mirrors God's image and likeness back to you. The more you exalt God in who he is, the more he unveils who you are to him and to the world. Empower yourself through personal praise and worship, corporate praise and worship, and allowing your life to be a lifestyle of ministry unto God.

11. **Lifelong Learner** – Possess a desire to know God and what pleases him. This is the reason we pray, study our word, and study other materials about God, because we want to know him – learn of him. Be a lifelong learner so all there is to know about your evolving God can be revealed to you.

12. **Accountability** - Being accountable to cultivating the relationship and to the promises and vows you make with God and with others. Do not make vows you cannot keep. If you struggle keeping them repent quickly, then seek God for deliverance and healing needed to keep that vow. You can also ask God to give you steps you can commit to, such that you work towards fulfilling a vow.

13. **Fidelity** - Be faithful to the relationship you have with God. Do not put things, people, situations, life pursuits, and idols in the place of God or ahead of God.

14. **Free will** - God does not make us be in relationship with him. He allows it to be our choice. God would rather be heartbroken with not having relationship with us, than to be dysfunctional in making us be in a relationship that we do not want to be in.

15. **SHIFT** – SHIFT to loving God with all of your heart, all of your mind, all of your soul. Do not fret! You will get there as you work on walking with him daily and letting him guide you in your destiny lifestyle. YOU GOT THIS! SHIFT!

Write a short paragraph encouraging yourself in SHIFTING your relationship with God to another level of covenant. Spend time thanking the Lord for wanting to journey in a destiny relationship with you.

_____
_____
_____
_____
_____
_____
_____
_____
_____
_____
_____
_____
_____
_____
_____
_____
_____
_____
_____
_____
_____
_____
_____
_____

BIBLICAL ENGRAVEMENTS OF VISION PLANS

(This chapter is from my book, "Healing The Wounded Leader.")

Isaiah 30:8 Now go, write it before them in a table, and note it in a book, that it may be for the time to come for ever and ever.

Written vision plans take what is spiritually stated, and physically engraves (imparts and establishes) it into the earth realm. It solidifies what God has spoken about you and that vision such that what he has already imparted in the earth about you connects with what he is further releasing about you in the spirit. As they meet, manifestation occurs, and evolves in helping your destiny to unfold in the earth. The Ten Commandments are a prime example of a Godly vision plan.

The Ten Commandments provided a clear written vision of how God wanted the Israelites to live (*See Exodus 20*). It was God's way of establishing a covenant bond with Israel as their Lord and savior, who delivered them from Egypt, and desired them to further live in redemption with him. They were engraved on tablets, so the Israelites could have the vision plan before them, while being physically established (engraved) in the earth.

Sampson

Sampson was given a vision plan for his life before he was conceived. This was a clear vision for keeping Sampson safe, blessed, anointed, strong, and powerful. If followed correctly, this plan would have enabled Sampson to successfully sustain in his destiny task as a deliverer of Israel.

Judges 13:3-5 And the angel of the Lord appeared unto the woman, and said unto her, Behold now, thou art barren, and bearest not: but thou shalt conceive, and bear a son. Now therefore beware, I pray thee, and drink not wine nor strong drink, and eat not any unclean thing: For, lo, thou shalt conceive, and bear a son; and no razor shall come on his head: for the child shall be a Nazarite unto God from the womb: and he shall begin to deliver Israel out of the hand of the Philistines.

Timothy

Timothy was provided a vision plan for his ministry. It was tailored to issues that were occurring in his congregation, and in the lives and marriages of the saints at that time. It was an example of how we are to have a specific vision plan that fit the needs, challenges, training, and development of our ministries.

1Timothy 1-4 I exhort therefore, that, first of all, supplications, prayers, intercessions, and giving of thanks, be made for all men; For kings, and for all that are in authority; that we may lead a quiet and peaceable life in all godliness and honesty. For this is good and acceptable in the sight of God our Saviour; Who will have all men to be saved, and to come unto the knowledge of the truth.

Verse 8-15 I will therefore that men pray every where, lifting up holy hands, without wrath and doubting. In like manner also, that women adorn themselves in modest apparel, with shamefacedness and sobriety; not with broided hair, or gold, or pearls, or costly array; But (which becometh women professing godliness) with good works. Let the woman learn in silence with all subjection. But I suffer not a woman to teach, nor to usurp authority over the man, but to be in silence. For Adam was first formed, then Eve. And Adam was not deceived, but the woman being deceived was in the transgression. Notwithstanding she shall be saved in childbearing, if they continue in faith and charity and holiness with sobriety.

John

John wrote a vision plan to prevent sin from occurring in the lives of the people he oversaw. He was making sure they knew how to avoid sin, and deal with sin should they fall.

1John 2:1-2 My little children, these things write I unto you, that ye sin not. And if any man sin, we have an advocate with the Father, Jesus Christ the righteous: And he is the propitiation for our sins: and not for ours only, but also for the sins of the whole world.

Peter

Peter provided a vision plan for walking in wellness and sustaining maturity of the Lord.

1Peter 1-25 So put away all malice and all deceit and hypocrisy and envy and all slander. Like newborn infants, long for the pure spiritual milk, that by it you may grow up into salvation – if indeed you have tasted that the Lord is good. As you come to him, a living stone rejected by men but in the sight of God chosen and precious, you yourselves like living stones are being built up as a spiritual house, to be a holy priesthood, to offer spiritual sacrifices acceptable to God through Jesus Christ....

Nicodemus

Jesus gave Nicodemus a personal vision plan for being born again.

John 3:1-21 There was a man of the Pharisees, named Nicodemus, a ruler of the Jews: The same came to Jesus by night, and said unto him, Rabbi, we know that thou art a teacher come from God: for no man can do these miracles that thou doest, except God be with him. Jesus answered and said unto him, Verily, verily, I say unto thee, Except a man be born again, he cannot see the kingdom of God. Nicodemus saith unto him, How can a man be born when he is old? can he enter the second time into his mother's womb, and be born? Jesus answered, Verily, verily, I say unto thee, Except a man be born of water and of the Spirit, he cannot enter into the kingdom of God. That which is born of the flesh is flesh; and that which is born of the Spirit is spirit. Marvel not that I said unto thee, Ye must be born again.....

We are to write the vision and make it plain:

Habakkuk 2:1-4 I will stand upon my watch, and set me upon the tower, and will watch to see what he will say unto me, and what I shall answer when I am reproved. And the Lord answered me, and said, Write the vision, and make it plain upon tables, that he may run that readeth it. For the vision is yet for an appointed time, but at the end it shall speak, and not lie: though it tarry, wait for it; because it will surely come, it will not tarry. Behold, his soul which is lifted up is not upright in him: but the just shall live by his faith.

Calendars & Journals are Accountability Plans

It is essential that leaders have calendars and journals. Trying to keep everything in your head causes stress, burnout, and memory loss. It also opens the door for you to appear inconsistent, immature, and unreliable due to missed appointments, and not being accountable to plans that you make vows to keep. Write everything down and keep dates and times of even small commitments so you can stick to working your vision plans, and being responsible and balanced in scheduling and attending appointments.

Even schedule your time with the Lord and other goals you are working on. God must be a priority. He must come first and everything else flows through him. Also, after your immediate family that lives in the house with you, what he requires of you comes next. So, schedule that in as well. As you take care of God's work, he will exceedingly take care of your work.

> *Matthew 19:29 And every one that hath forsaken houses, or brethren, or sisters, or father, or mother, or wife, or children, or lands, for my name's sake, shall receive a hundredfold, and shall inherit everlasting life.*

> *Matthew 6:33 But seek first the kingdom of God and His righteousness, and all these things will be added unto you.*

<u>*Vision Plans Can:*</u>

- ✓ Be Seasonal (specifically and strategically focused on where you are in your life and ministry)

- ✓ Specific in Assignment (strategic to a goal you and/or God wants you to obtain)

- ✓ Personal or Ministerial (tailored to your personal life or ministry - both are needed as a leader)

- ✓ Specific to Deliverance and Healing or Personal Growth and Development (tailored to current sin issues, character flaws, generational strongholds, cycles and habits, training and development needed to mature in one's gifts and callings, ministerial and personal growth, etc.)

- ✓ Strategic to Walking in Sustaining Destiny:
  - ❖ What is your purpose and calling?
  - ❖ What is God revealing concerning your purpose and calling?

- ❖ What is God requiring of you at this season of your destiny?

- ❖ What character traits, connections, disciplines, and accountability measures do you need to fulfill what God is requiring in this current season?

- ❖ What type of relationships, acquaintanceships, connections, covering, mentorship is beneficial to your destiny walk (e.g. What do you need from a spouse, what type of friends, acquaintances, connections do you need, what is your standard for marriage, friendships, acquaintances, connections; what type of covering/mentorship do you need, what is your standard for a healthy covering and/or mentoring relationship?

- ❖ What is God requiring from you daily, weekly, seasonally as it relates to respite, personal prayer, and study time that is specifically focused on you, lifestyle and seasons of fasting and consecration (e.g. Take Monday's for personal time, every two months take a vacation, fast two days a week, every quarter do a 21 day fast, take time off from all ministry the entire month of December).

- ❖ Standards are not just morals and values, as morals and values can be good, decent, and respectful, but lack Godly principles and standards. Though Jesus fulfilled the law, there are still statutes we have to abide by that demonstrate that we belong to God and his kingdom (*read Matthew 5:16-21*). Now that we have our own personal relationship with God through the works of Jesus Christ, what God may require of you may be different than what God is requiring of someone else. Standards are tailor made biblical principles that align with the word of God, while enabling us to hold fast the profession of our faith. Standards keep you from transgressing against the character, nature, virtue, maturity, discipline, faith and steadfastness God is requiring for your life. What are the standards God is requiring of you, such that you sustain your journey in a successful destiny lifestyle with the Lord?

Hebrews 4:14-16 Seeing then that we have a great high priest, that is passed into the heavens, Jesus the Son of God, let us hold fast our profession. For we have not a high priest which cannot be touched with the feeling of our infirmities; but was in all points tempted like as we are, yet without sin. Let us therefore come boldly unto the throne of grace, that we may obtain mercy, and find grace to help in time of need.

When God requires us to birth a vision in the earth, we become known as his vision carriers. Every biblical character mentioned above was a vision carrier. Like you, they embodied the spiritual and natural ability to carry, birth, plant, plow, build, and establish God's plan and purpose in the earth; whether that be via ministry, business, organization, school, college, center, club, book, etc. This vision is instilled at birth. And God gives clear instructions to the vision carrier for how to bring the vision to pass. The vision is not meant to be a burden. It can feel like a burden when we:

- Are not aware that we are vision carriers

- Do not embrace the vision such that we become the vision
- Reject the vision
- Waver in the vision
- Are not clear or able to visibly see or understand the purpose of the vision
- Strive to bring the vision to pass without a relationship with God or without direction from God
- Are weary and need rest from the duties and tasks as a vision carrier
- Are in intense seasons of planting, plowing, building, or in seasons of warfare – know that this is just for a season and will lift as you solidify and conquer through the work God has ordained for that season
- Battling a destiny killing spirit/s who desires to destroy the vision – you must identity and break the powers of this/these spirits over your life. We will discuss this in a later chapter

Please know who God calls, he has equipped. He has equipped you as a vision carrier.

Romans 8:29-31 For whom he did foreknow, he also did predestinate to be conformed to the image of his Son, that he might be the firstborn among many brethren. Moreover whom he did predestinate, them he also called: and whom he called, them he also justified: and whom he justified, them he also glorified. What shall we then say to these things? If God be for us, who can be against us?

Write a decree regarding how God has predestined you, called you, justified you, and equipped you for his glory. Verbally declare your decree over your life for a week straight.

_____
_____
_____
_____
_____
_____
_____
_____
_____
_____
_____
_____
_____
_____
_____
_____
_____
_____
_____
_____

WISDOM KEYS FOR ACCOUNTABILITY TO VISION PLANS

- Plans should be consistently revisited and reevaluated before the Lord, and only changed or demolished at his leading.
- Plans should be consistently worked and invested into before totally revamping a plan. Give God your best effort at working a plan so even if it needs changing, you are being accountable to what he is requiring of you.
- If the Lord tells you to get rid of a plan, scrap it immediately. He will give you a more efficient plan that is in line with where you are and what he is doing, or he may have you return to that plan at a later time in your destiny journey.
- Consider an accountability partner to help you remain disciplined in working your vision plan. This person should be invested in your personal and spiritual walk, and be able to intercede and carry you in the spirit.
- Even if you and God decide to totally revamp a vision plan, spend time self-evaluating before the Lord. Examine what was good and bad about the vision, successful and unsuccessful about the vision, areas you did or did not follow through, disciplines needed to fulfill the plan, the reason you are revamping, what you will do differently with your new plan. Repent for any areas of sin, disobedience, failures, and where you dropped the ball. Spend time fasting, consecrating, and spiritually building yourself up in the character, integrity, accountability, and disciplines you need before starting your new vision plan (e.g. Standing on scriptures and decrees that build your confidence and identity, praying and fasting against personal and generational curses, strongholds, cycles and habits, receiving training in areas related to the success of the vision).

Journal what you learned regarding the biblical foundations of vision plans and the reason it is essential to have clear vision, write the vision, and journey with God in producing the vision in the earth.

_____
_____
_____
_____
_____
_____
_____
_____
_____
_____
_____
_____
_____
_____
_____
_____

Journal the reason it is important to be accountable to your vision plan.

KNOWING YOUR DESTINY VISION

To successfully release your vision, you must first know your calling and purpose for being in the earth. Destiny and vision go hand and hand in fulfilling the call of God on your life.

Dictionary.com defines *calling* as:
1. vocation, profession, or trade, what is your calling?
2. to summon by or as if by divine command he felt called to the ministry
3. to summon to an office, duty, etc.
4. to designate as something specified

Merriam-Webster's Dictionary defines *destiny* as:
1. what happens in the future, the things that someone or something will experience in the future
2. a power that is believed to control what happens in the future
3. something to which a person or thing is destined, fortune
4. a predetermined course of events often held to be an irresistible power or agency
5. synonyms see fate

Merriam-Webster's Dictionary defines *vision* as:
1. the ability to see, sight or eyesight
2. something that you imagine, a picture that you see in your mind
3. something that you see or dream, especially as part of a religious or supernatural experience
4. something seen in a dream, trance, or ecstasy, especially a supernatural appearance that conveys a revelation

My definition:
- *Calling* is what you are anointed or appointed to do.
- *Destiny* is where we are going in life. Destiny is a progressive journey with God. We all have destiny moments of success, but destiny is a lifestyle journey with the Lord.
- *Vision* is the journey and plans our lives will take to operate in our calling and achieve destiny.

Destiny Scriptures:

Genesis 1:26-28 And God said, Let us make man in our image, after our likeness: and let them have dominion over the fish of the sea, and over the fowl of the air, and over the cattle, and over all the earth, and over every creeping thing that creepeth upon the earth. So God created man in his own image, in the image of God created he him; male and female created he them. And God blessed them, and God said unto them, Be fruitful, and multiply, and replenish the earth, and subdue it: and have dominion over the fish of the sea, and over the fowl of the air, and over every living thing that moveth upon the earth.

Proverbs 19:21 *Many plans are in a man's mind, but it is the Lord's purpose for him that will stand.*

Psalm 119:105 *Your word is a lamp to my feet, and a light to my path.*

Psalms 139:13-17 *For thou hast possessed my reins: thou hast covered me in my mother's womb. I will praise thee; for I am fearfully and wonderfully made: marvellous are thy works; and that my soul knoweth right well. My substance was not hid from thee, when I was made in secret, and curiously wrought in the lowest parts of the earth. Thine eyes did see my substance, yet being unperfect; and in thy book all my members were written, which in continuance were fashioned, when as yet there was none of them. How precious also are thy thoughts unto me, O God! How great is the sum of them!*

Jeremiah 29:11 *- For I know the thoughts that I think toward you, saith the LORD, thoughts of peace, and not of evil, to give you an expected end.*

Jeremiah 1:5 *- Before I formed thee in the belly I knew thee; and before thou camest forth out of the womb I sanctified thee, [and] I ordained thee a prophet unto the nations.*

Let's explore the distinction between gifts and talents.

Talents

Talents are skills and abilities that you do well. All talents are not listed in the bible, but are a grace, uniqueness, and ability to do something with supernatural uniqueness and ability that others may or may not have, and even if they do have it, it is not a prototype of you or your talent. An example of talents would be playing the piano, a musical instrument, singing, being a great athlete, being a genius, skilled at math, etc. If you do it well and it comes naturally to you, it is probably a talent that God supernaturally gifted you with.

Gifts

Spiritual gifts are in the bible. They are gifts empowered in us through God's Holy Spirit. They are gifts that God has given for the purposes of saving the lost, bringing deliverance and healing to people, lands, and regions, and establishing God's kingdom in the earth.

Spiritual Gifts in the bible:

Romans 12:6-8	1 Corinthians 12:8-10	1 Corinthians 12:28
• Prophecy • Serving • Teaching • Exhortation • Giving	• Word of wisdom • Word of knowledge • Faith	• Apostle • Prophet • Teacher • Miracles

• Leadership • Mercy	• Gifts of healings • Miracles • Prophecy • Distinguishing between spirits • Tongues • Interpretation of tongues	• Kinds of healings • Helps • Administration • Tongues

Romans 12:6-8 *Having then gifts differing according to the grace that is given to us, whether prophecy, let us prophesy according to the proportion of faith; Or ministry, let us wait on our ministering: or he that teacheth, on teaching; Or he that exhorteth, on exhortation: he that giveth, let him do it with simplicity; he that ruleth, with diligence; he that sheweth mercy, with cheerfulness.*

1Corinthians 12: 8-10 *For to one is given by the Spirit the word of wisdom; to another the word of knowledge by the same Spirit; To another faith by the same Spirit; to another the gifts of healing by the same Spirit; To another the working of miracles; to another prophecy; to another discerning of spirits; to another divers kinds of tongues; to another the interpretation of tongues:*

1Corinthians 12:28-31 *And God hath set some in the church, first apostles, secondarily prophets, thirdly teachers, after that miracles, then gifts of healings, helps, governments, diversities of tongues. Are all apostles? are all prophets? are all teachers? are all workers of miracles? Have all the gifts of healing? do all speak with tongues? do all interpret? But covet earnestly the best gifts: and yet shew I unto you a more excellent way.*

You can ask the Holy Spirit to give you these gifts and he can teach you how to operate in them. As you grow in these gifts, you can become skilled in using them.

Governmental Offices

Ephesians 4:11
• Apostle • Prophet • Evangelist • Pastor • Teacher

Ephesians 4:11-13 *And he gave some, apostles; and some, prophets; and some, evangelists; and some, pastors and teachers; For the perfecting of the saints, for the work of the ministry, for the edifying of the body of Christ: Till we all come in the unity of the faith, and of the*

knowledge of the Son of God, unto a perfect man, unto the measure of the stature of the fulness of Christ.

These are governmental offices that God gave as gifts for the equipping of the body of Christ. God installs these offices in you at birth. If he does not install this office in you, you cannot promote yourself to this office or go to a Christian school, learn these gifts, then be positioned into these offices. Either they are in you or they are not. These offices are for the purposes of providing spiritual authorities that can empower, equip, and release the body of Christ in their giftings and callings, while asserting and maintaining Godly jurisdiction against principalities and strongholds that would strive to bind people, lands, and regions. A person can be apostolic, prophetic, evangelistic, etc., but not operate in a governmental office. The office provides you the ability to govern and legislate against demonic entities, spiritual realms, regions, and within the constructs of assemblies, businesses, and communities. If God has not called you to this, you can encounter a lot of hardship and tribulation by putting yourself in these positions as those who have the offices, have a grace to contend and endure the warfare that comes with these offices.

> ***2Corinthians 4:8-17*** *We are troubled on every side, yet not distressed; we are perplexed, but not in despair; Persecuted, but not forsaken; cast down, but not destroyed; Always bearing about in the body the dying of the Lord Jesus, that the life also of Jesus might be made manifest in our body. For we which live are always delivered unto death for Jesus' sake, that the life also of Jesus might be made manifest in our mortal flesh. So then death worketh in us, but life in you. We having the same spirit of faith, according as it is written, I believed, and therefore have I spoken; we also believe, and therefore speak; Knowing that he which raised up the Lord Jesus shall raise up us also by Jesus, and shall present us with you. For all things are for your sakes, that the abundant grace might through the thanksgiving of many redound to the glory of God. For which cause we faint not; but though our outward man perish, yet the inward man is renewed day by day. For our light affliction, which is but for a moment, worketh for us a far more exceeding and eternal weight of glory; While we look not at the things which are seen, but at the things which are not seen: for the things which are seen are temporal; but the things which are not seen are eternal.*

Though as saints, we endure some of this for the gospel sake, those in governmental offices live this daily as a lifestyle and mandate. It can be a constant spiritual and natural battle depending on what season of destiny they are in. Imagine striving to endure this type of lifestyle warfare daily without God creating you for this position? It would be a horrific life of unnecessary hardship.

I also want to say that if God called you to these offices and you do not embrace them, you can have warfare. The principalities and powers in these jurisdictions are contending and waring for these realms and you will feel and experience the weight of that whether you embrace your gifted office or not. Your ability to contend and tower in the grace God has given you over these entities is to SHIFT into your rightful office and establish the authority God has given you to govern over darkness within your spheres of influences.

Sevenfold Spirit Of The Lord

In addition to being born with talents and gifts, born in gifted offices, and pursuing supernatural gifts, the Spirit of the Lord can rest upon you with an anointing and qualification to judge through the intellect and mind of God.

Isaiah 11:2 And the spirit of the Lord shall rest upon him, the spirit of wisdom and understanding, the spirit of counsel and might, the spirit of knowledge and of the fear of the Lord. And shall make him of quick understanding in the fear of the Lord: and he shall not judge after the sight of his eyes, neither reprove after the hearing of his ears: But with righteousness shall he judge the poor, and reprove with equity for the meek of the earth: and he shall smite the earth: with the rod of his mouth, and with the breath of his lips shall he slay the wicked.

Gifts Make Room

Proverbs 18:12 says, "A man's gift maketh room for him, and bringeth him before great men."

We tend to equate this scripture to our capabilities and talents. However, the word *gift* in this scripture means, *"offerings, presents, reward, gift."* It is really when we are giving our gifts as a blessing to others that makes room for us and SHIFTS us into greatness. This is essential to recognizing that our gifts and talents have purpose. They are to empower someone's life, the earth, and the world at large. We must pursue God for how he desires us to impact others, the earth, and the world, so we can be the greatest person he desired us to be. SHIFT!

Gifts Versus Destiny

One of the revelations I have received is that destiny is not a gift or talent, it is a function of your purpose and calling. We can narrow down what our destiny may be by what we do well, but that does not necessarily mean that is the function of our destiny. This is the reason it is important for parents to begin asking God what their child's purpose and calling is in the earth. As most times, children are groomed in their gifts and talents - what they do well, and the assumption is "this is their destiny and calling. Some people stumble upon or into destiny and some strive to pursue a desired dream, or a portion of destiny based on personal aptitudes and strengths that may or may not unveil or SHIFT them into destiny.

Take myself for example. I was supported in my talents, but not groomed in the function of destiny. As a young child, I was very smart. I loved to dance so for several years, my aunt had me attending different genres of dance classes. After learning how to play basketball, I stopped attending dance classes and started attending basketball camps, clubs and the like. I played basketball all throughout junior high, high school, and into college. I was not groomed for college though I was encouraged to go to college. I surely was not groomed for a career or destiny. I was groomed to go to church, survive, be strong, persevere, never give up, be a woman that did not need anyone for anything, stand on my own two feet, have great work ethic, be the best that I can be and to take care of myself. These attributes were engrained in me, and have helped sustain me in destiny, but did not help me to know my destiny.

In college, I chose the major psychology because I was always intrigued by why people do what they do. After undergrad, I pursued a counseling degree as I was wise, a good listener, and could help people solve life problems. This became my career path and what I thought was my destiny, so I began to walk in it. I have had numerous counseling and case management jobs, but I have spent much of my professional career in the job function of a behavior consultant. Professionally, I do perform some counseling, but mostly I provide consultation and skills building to mentally and physically challenged people of all ages. This would have been my destiny path, had I not entered a relationship with Jesus, and realized that counseling is a judgment gift that rest upon me, consultation is a talent, but this is not my destiny.

As I really became saved and began to journey with Jesus as a lifestyle, everything I thought about my life began to SHIFT. Aside from obtaining a master's degree, much of what I thought was my destiny path and what I would accomplish in life, has never unfolded. And what God has revealed and caused me to do in life was never my expectation or anything I would have chosen or fathomed for myself. I would have never chosen any of this because I was not groomed in relationship with God, I was groomed to go to church. I was not groomed to seek God in destiny nor that was my destiny rooted in God.

As I journeyed in relationship with God, I still stumbled into my destiny. Though I consistently attended church and utilized my gifts, talents, and strengths in church, I was not groomed in destiny. Actually, I was the only one talking about the importance of destiny at the church I attended. But works, talent and position, were the forefront of the church, so it was very difficult to get anyone to really listen and cultivate a lifestyle of destiny into us as sheep.

My obedience to whatever God told me to do and what he revealed and unveiled as I journeyed with him, SHIFTED me into destiny. I did not even know this was what was unfolding until I was committed to God. I possessed a yearning that all I wanted to do was please God and be in his will. Then I began to realize that what he was having me to do as we walked through life in covenant together, was my destiny lifestyle and I were walking out my life's purpose in him. By that time, I was preaching, teaching, delivering, healing, and saving others, while helping them to explore and SHIFT into their destiny and life's purpose. The more I walked in this, the more my purpose was revealed and became defined. I also learned how to pursue gifts of the Holy Spirit and use them to empower the talents and skills that were within me. Because I did not know until I was doing destiny, that my destiny and calling was being identified, I had many seasons where I just called myself a humble servant, then I slowly took on the title of minister, then I thought, and others called me a prophet, then I learned and realized through the counsel and direction of God that I was an Apostle and that my calling was to raise up kingdom shifters for his glory. Had I been groomed to journey with God in relationship, I could have bypassed a lot of trials, seasons of the unknowns, error, etc., and been groomed in destiny from a young age.

Even as an Apostle, I use my counseling gift that rest upon me to judge, but it is not the sum total of me. It is only a fraction of my destiny - not the consumption. I believe this is the reason many famous people are so unfulfilled. They have pursued their dreams and get to operate and succeed in their gifts and talents, but that is not their full purpose in life - it is not the consumption of them. After they have attained a measure of success, many of them are still empty as they strive to find real purpose. Without a relationship with God, many engage in a lot of good works and services of helping others through their financial wealth, giving encouraging talks and taking on causes through their famous platforms, but rarely is this purpose or fulfilling. And we wonder how someone with lots of money, can buy and have whatever they want, can still be lonely, unfulfilled, constantly error or have trials, lack focus and platforms sustainment, etc. it is because what they are doing and have done all their lives is not destiny. It is works of gifting but not works of destiny. Because God created us, and we are made in his image, we cannot successfully journey in our destiny and calling without a relationship with him. Without a relationship with God, our talents and gifts can produce success and prosperity, but it will not produce destiny fulfillment. Destiny fulfillment can only come from journeying with God in a destiny lifestyle.

>**Proverbs 19:21** *There are many devices in a man's heart; nevertheless the counsel of the LORD, that shall stand.*

<u>Devices</u> in the Hebrew is *mahašăbâ* or *machashebeth* and means:
1. contrivance (plots, schemes, plans), i.e. (concretely) a texture
2. machine (workings), or (abstractly) intention,
3. plan (whether bad, a plot; or good, advice): — cunning (work), curious work
4. device(-sed), imagination, invented, means, purpose, thought/s

- ✓ Good thoughts, ideas, and plans do not equate to destiny.
- ✓ Good imaginations and dreams do not equate to destiny.
- ✓ Good plans, cunning and curious works, plots and schemes do not equate to destiny.
- ✓ Good works and working hard while producing great success do not equate to destiny.
- ✓ Just because you thought it and it produced does not equate to destiny.

>**New American Standard Bible** *There are many plans in a man's heart; nevertheless the counsel of the LORD that shall stand.*

If it is not the thoughts and mind of God for you, it is not destiny.

>**Jeremiah 29:11** *For I know the thoughts that I think toward you, saith the LORD, thoughts of peace, and not of evil, to give you an expected end.*

The word *thoughts* in this scripture is the same word as *devices* in **Proverbs 19:21**. God's thoughts that must govern our lives. You cannot do this without relationship with him – your creator.

Your function may be minister, business owner, counselor, Pastor, CEO, Prophet, Psalmist, etc., and there are great giftings and talents intertwined in these areas, but make sure you are in purpose and not talented and gifted works. You can work a gift or talent and not be in destiny or in purpose. Purpose gives the gift and talent meaning and fulfillment. Purpose is what enables us to walk in, unveil, and evolve in destiny. You do not want to leave this world being known as a good person who did a lot of great things and touched a lot of people but never fulfilled destiny.

> **Proverbs 19:21** *The Message Version We humans keep brainstorming options and plans, but God's purpose prevails.*

It is vital that parents SHIFT to grooming their children to walk in destiny at a young age by teaching them a relationship with God and to hear God for their destiny and purpose. Teach children to hear God for purpose and begin to groom them in loving God so that they will want to live for him and do what he says.

It is vital that the church SHIFT to grooming people in having a relationship with God and hearing him for destiny, while empowering, equipping, and releasing people in a lifestyle of destiny and purpose.

We need to stop wasting precious time investing and engaging in frivolous works that produce little to no fruit in the earth, and that keep us apart from God, and his ordained will for our lives. What is in our heart can and will unfold if we pursue it, but that does not mean this is destiny. We need the counsel of the Lord to attain the true plans for our lives. You can get his counsel and plans through relationship, and allowing him to guide your life's journey. When God guides you, your destiny and calling can stand and withstand the test of times.

When something is standing, it:
- Is able to be independent.
- Is able to endure without supports.
- Is grounded in a strong foundation.
- Is a pillar.
- Reveals and exposes.
- Speaks for itself through its stance.
- Represents and confirms the purpose of that which erected it.
- Demonstrates strength and durability.
- Establishes its intent and purpose in the earth.

When your destiny can stand and withstand the tests of time, they are able to give him glory throughout generations.

Psalms 145:4 *One generation shall praise thy works to another, and shall declare thy mighty acts.*

Who are you?

_____
_____
_____
_____
_____
_____
_____
_____
_____
_____
_____
_____
_____
_____
_____
_____
_____
_____
_____
_____

Who does God say you are?

_____
_____
_____
_____
_____
_____
_____
_____
_____
_____
_____
_____
_____
_____
_____
_____
_____

What is the calling upon your life?

What is the purpose of the calling upon your life?

What about your calling makes you unique in the earth?

What are your talents, gifts, offices if any apply? What judging gifts of Godly intellect rest upon you?

Ask God how does he desire to utilize your giftings and callings to impact his kingdom and the world?

HOW TO WRITE A PERSONAL DESTINY PLAN

It is essential to have a personal destiny plan. This will enable you to remain accountable to the standards and biblical truths God has set for your life. This plan will enable you to sustain in destiny, while being fortified to carry the vision he has granted to your hands. Your plan may be different than someone else's. God knows what your standards need to be and what path you need to take to be successful in your destiny walk and to maintain progress in every season of your life.

This is an example of my personal destiny plan. It is very strict, but tailored to me.

Vision For My Standards: You are my representation of unwavering faith and wholeness. Pursue and strive to live a lifestyle of holiness, righteousness, purity and virtue. This is essential for operating in the raw power and strong anointing of God, and for keeping doors closed to sin, unnecessary drama, and hardship.

Vision Accountability Points:

- Only date for marriage. Seek me for the standard of the mate you are to marry and a standard for dating. Never settle from this standard.
- Seek me for the standard of personal friends you should have; keep your personal life guarded from people that may not value and operate in this same standard.
- Seek me for a heart to hate the things I hate and love the things I love.
- Do not watch movies, listen to music, attend events, or entertain conversations that entails perversion, gossip/slander of others, witchcraft, and blaspheme or dishonor God.
- Be a lifelong learner and pursuer of being trained and equipped in your destiny and calling, but be spirit led in what and who you receive from.
- Seek me before attending any church events, trainings, conferences, etc. This will assist with not opening the doors to tainted impartations that can cause defilement.
- Maintain a consistent weekly fasting regimen and seek me for quarterly personal fasts and consecrations (March, June, September). This is in addition to ministry fasts and consecrations, and seasons of strategic fasting and consecrations.
- Guard your mouth and be quick to repent, as what you speak could release word curses.
- Guard your eye and ear gates as they can be door openers to demonic dreams and ungodly dream impartations.
- Repent quickly and consistently check in with the Holy Spirit to make sure you have his conviction.
- Check yourself for humility such that how I use you will not become a stumbling post for pride.
- Forgive quickly and seek to resolve conflict quickly. Bring me your true feelings. Be open to releasing them to me so you can heal and resolve matters in a Godly manner.
- Be a life pursuer of personal deliverance and healing. Know that it is a part of your destiny walk with me.

- Do not participate in pagan holidays. Remember, this is just an example however, God will tailor your standards in what is best for you. e.g. Sampson could not cut his hair as it cut off his strength. Pagan holidays are rooted in idolatry. Idolatry breeds defilement, and paganism opens the door to idolatry and sin.
- Do not take risks that will lend to sin and transgressions. Know what you can and cannot handle and be okay with not being able to handle or do things others do. Understand your risks based on your background and the generational strongholds in your family line. For example: You were a heavy drinker in the world and come from a line of alcoholics; so even social drinking is a risk you do not need to take as it could lend to drinking when stressed, overburdened, or to being addicted to alcohol.
- Eat healthy and exercise three times a week - Explore the generational health challenges in your family line, and seek me for a personal health plan to break curses. Minimize your pork and dairy intake and consume lots of fruits and veggies. This will help you sustain in strength, vitality, and wellness, while avoiding generational sicknesses that cut off the life span.

What is your perception of destiny?

_____
_____
_____
_____
_____
_____
_____
_____
_____
_____
_____
_____
_____
_____
_____
_____
_____
_____
_____

What challenges have you endured in striving to walk in destiny?

_____
_____
_____
_____

What emotional challenges and fears do you have regarding destiny?

Who have been your biggest supporters in your destiny walk? Explain your answer.

Who have been your biggest discouragers in your destiny walk? Explain your answer?

What personal deliverance and healing do you need at this point in your destiny walk?

WRITING YOUR PERSONAL DESTINY VISION PLAN

Why is a personal vision plan necessary for you to walk in your destiny and calling with the Lord? Include specific reasons.

_____
_____
_____
_____
_____
_____
_____
_____
_____
_____
_____
_____
_____
_____
_____
_____
_____
_____
_____

Ask God for a personal vision plan to help you fulfill your destiny? Journal what he says.

_____
_____
_____
_____
_____
_____
_____
_____
_____
_____
_____
_____
_____
_____
_____

Write your destiny plan in the format of the example I gave for my personal destiny plan:

____

Vision For My Standards:

____

Vision Accountability Points:

____

GOD DESIRES US TO PROSPER!

1Samuel 2:6-10 The Lord killeth, and maketh alive: he bringeth down to the grave, and bringeth up. The Lord maketh poor, and maketh rich: he bringeth low, and lifteth up. He raiseth up the poor out of the dust, and lifteth up the beggar from the dunghill, to set them among princes, and to make them inherit the throne of glory: for the pillars of the earth are the Lord's, and he hath set the world upon them.

He will keep the feet (journey) of his saints, and the wicked shall be silent in darkness; for by strength shall no man prevail. The adversaries of the Lord shall be broken to pieces (Hebrew word Hatat and means shattered, broken down, beat down, amazed, dismayed, terrified, abolished); out of heaven shall he thunder upon them: the Lord shall judge the ends of the earth; and he shall give strength unto his king, and exalt the horn of his anointed. **SHIFT!**

Marketplace ministry typically refers to entrepreneurial endeavors that have a Christian kingdom foundation targeting business ventures, the secular workplace, community organizations, regional and political influence, and specialized venues (e.g., crusades). It can also refer to particular parachurch organizations, hubs, centers, clubs, schools, universities that are geared towards spiritually empowering, equipping, training, and educating people and systems. These marketplace ministries are for profit or non-for-profit depending on the services rendered.

Many Christians have been led to believe that we are not to be paid for our giftings and services. It has been engrained in us that to require payment for giftings and services is considered pimping God and his people. And because we have seen many saints do just that, we do not want to be placed in that category.

The challenge with that is, God has instilled huge dreams and visions within us. What he has ordained for our lives is tied to the very giftings we freely give to ministries and people on the daily basis. Also, these giftings are a part of our destiny, but because we generally focus on acquiring an education and career based on our talents, rarely do we have a mindset regarding destiny, and how our destiny is to unfold in the earth. It is my hope that this book will SHIFT you into identifying your destiny, identifying your giftings, and assisting you with releasing your entrepreneurial vision productively as God has designed for your life.

It is important to note that though God does not want money or anything else to take his place in our lives, God desires us to prosper. Even in our non-for-profit endeavors, God desires us to be blessed. He wants to always be God and our head, and he wants us to be blessed. He does not want money or anything else to trump his presence and position in our lives. He does not want you to abuse people and ourselves by having money lead our lives. But he does want us to prosper and to be blessed.

***1Timothy 6:10** For the love of money is the root of all evil: which while some coveted after, they have erred from the faith, and pierced themselves through with many sorrows.*

Greek word for *pierced* is *peripeiro* and means *"penetrate entirely, pierce through, to torture one's soul with sorrow, to torture."*

God did not say money was evil, he said the love of money was evil. We discern here that when we fall in love with money, we become erred in our actions and stray away from God. We begin to covet such that we give ourselves up to obtaining money and the pangs and stressors that come with striving for money. God does not desire this for us, but please know that God does desire us to prosper.

> *Ecclesiastes 5:19* *Every man also to whom God hath given riches and wealth, and hath given him power to eat thereof, and to take his portion, and to rejoice in his labor; this is the gift of God.*

> *3John 3:2* *Beloved, I wish above all things that thou mayest prosper and be in health, even as thy soul prospereth.*

> *Psalms 90:17* *And let the beauty of the LORD our God be upon us: and establish thou the work of our hands upon us; yea, the work of our hands establish thou it.*

> *Deuteronomy 8:18* *But thou shalt remember the LORD thy God: for it is he that giveth thee power to get wealth, that he may establish his covenant which he sware unto thy fathers, as it is this day.*

When I first grasped this revelation, I recognized that much of the reason I had not experienced a sufficient portioned harvest was because I had not positioned myself for it. I was too busy being the good little servant who allowed people to take advantage of me rather than knowing my worth, and expecting provision and prosperity to be a part of my destiny walk and relationship with God.

- ✓ God cannot reproduce and multiply from seeds that have been sown in a false sense of humility or false loyalty.
- ✓ He cannot build a harvest upon seeds that have been given away through the guise of manipulation of others who would use our hearts and Christian faith to receive a product from us for free that they would gladly pay someone down the street for.
- ✓ God cannot bring increase to a seed that we never planted because we are too busy continuing to work the vision of others out of false loyalty and obligation, or fear of leaving the familiar, when our season of this has ended, and God is SHIFTING us into investing our time, focus, energy, resources, gifts, finances, into what he has personally ordained to our hands. I hear the Lord saying, *"What is in your hands Moses? What is in your hands?"*

> *Exodus 4:1-2* *And Moses answered and said, But, behold, they will not believe me, nor hearken unto my voice: for they will say, The Lord hath not appeared unto thee. And the Lord said unto him, What is that in thine hand? And he said, A rod.*

One of the Hebrew definitions of *rod* is *mattah or mate* and means *"a support of life."* Moses had everything in his hands to support the calling on his life, yet he had difficulty grasping his value and worth. Therefore, he could not adequately discern what God had put in him, and what God had equipped him with. Again, I ask, "*What is in your hand Moses? What is in your hands?*" **SHIFT!**

We have to understand that what is in our hand is our vision – our life's dream - our support. God has given us this rod to produce his kingdom and to produce wealth, so that we can be lenders and helpers of his kingdom and to the world. Our vision is a seed and if we never plant it, cultivate it, and work in sustaining its production, we thwart our own harvest and generational inheritance.

> ***1Corinthians 2:10** And [God] Who provides seed for the sower and bread for eating will also provide and multiply your [resources for] sowing and increase the fruits of your righteousness [which manifests itself in active goodness, kindness, and charity].*

Take a moment to meditate on this prayer and receive an impartation of Mattah. SHIFT!

Decreeing the revelation and action of the Mattah comes upon you even now. Decreeing that you know that the dreams, visions, books, ideas, that God has given you is a seed - a support of life. Decreeing that you possess the zeal of the Holy Spirit and instead of carrying that seed around in your heart and mind, you SHIFT to seeking God for the miracle working revelation and action to plant, nurture, cultivate, and sustain that seed where it becomes generational harvest to you and your lineage. SHIFT!

Most businesses, organizations, ministries, books, etc., start with no money. They start with an idea - a premise, and then the visionary makes the necessary sacrifices to invest and work that idea to bring their vision to past.

> ***Proverbs 8:12** I wisdom dwell with prudence and find out knowledge of witty inventions.*

Inventions is *mezimaˆ* in the Hebrew and means *"a purpose, plan, device, or discretion - which is the right or power to make decisions."*

It is important for us to learn what God wants for us, what we want for ourselves, seek God for how to bring that to pass, and act in working what he says.

> ***Jeremiah 29:11** For I know the thoughts that I think toward you, saith the Lord, thoughts of peace, and not of evil, to give you an expected end.*

<u>Thoughts</u> in the Hebrew is *machashebeth* and means:
1. a contrivance (plan or force), i.e. (concretely) a texture, machine, or (abstractly) intention, plan (whether bad, a plot; or good, advice)
2. cunning (work), curious work, device, imagination, invented, means, purpose, thought

> ***Psalms 19:21** Many are the plans in a person's heart, but it is the LORD's purpose that prevails.*

Isaiah 14:22 *The LORD Almighty has sworn, "Surely, as I have planned, so it will be, and as I have purposed, so it will happen.*

Psalms 37:4 *Delight thyself also in the LORD; and he shall give thee the desires of thine heart.*

In what ways did this chapter enlighten you about your giftings, entrepreneurial vision, and God's desire for you to prosper?

_____
_____
_____
_____
_____
_____
_____
_____
_____
_____
_____
_____
_____
_____
_____
_____
_____
_____

In what ways have you used your gifts and callings for God, and felt more like you were being taken advantage of by people or the church system than really being valued for your abilities and who you are in the earth? Spend time forgiving where necessary and declaring out your right to be blessed by who you are and what God has placed in your hands. Journal the impact of your prayer time in this area.

_____
_____
_____
_____
_____
_____
_____
_____
_____
_____
_____
_____

MONEY! MONEY! MONEY! MONEY!

My encouragement to you is that as you make money, do not be so quick to spend it. Sow it back into your vision so you can continue to grow and advance your market place endeavor. This sounds easy, but many find it very difficult to do. The focus is generally on being excited to have extra streams of income and ways to purchase material goods rather than investing. To assist with developing a healthy mindset regarding money and investments, it would be good to examine any challenging mindsets you have about money. Otherwise, the decisions you make regarding money can influence the growth, maturity, and integrity of your entrepreneurial vision and even your destiny.

What were the mindsets concerning money in your home when you were growing up? Were they frivolous, tightwads, generous, stressed regarding money, etc.?

_____
_____
_____
_____
_____
_____
_____
_____
_____
_____
_____
_____
_____
_____
_____
_____
_____
_____

How did your parents handle money? Did they invest? Did they pay their bills? Did they live from paycheck to paycheck?

_____
_____
_____
_____
_____
_____

What are the strongholds in your family line against members being able to flourish in jobs, businesses, and riches? Ask God to break these strongholds and any way you feel obligated to save or rescue the family from poverty, yet they are not striving to make healthy choices about their finances and credit.

What did you learn about money and what mindsets do you have about money that stem from your childhood?

What vows did you make regarding money as it relates to your childhood experiences? (e.g. I will never be broke, I will give my child everything, I will leave an inheritance for my children.)

How do you handle money now? How is your credit? What do you need to do to improve your credit? Be honest so that God can deal with you in this area. As things are revealed to you, journal your thoughts and feelings in this area. Repent and break curses and bondages as necessary.

What are the good and bad mindsets and behaviors that you have about money, finances, tithing, sowing, reaping, harvest?

Search with God for a plan of how you need to handle money to be integral in your entrepreneurial endeavors. Journal what he says. Practice this plan as money flows in from your vision.

___

Ask God to minister to you about what HE desires for you and your generations regarding prosperity as this will aide in breaking down poverty mindsets and hinderances to SHIFTING into market place ministry.

WRITING YOUR ENTREPRENEURIAL VISION PLAN!

As a vision carrier, your entrepreneurial vision plan consists of the missions and purposes God has provided to help you launch and establish the ministry, business, organization, school, college, center, club, book, etc. that he has given you. Your entrepreneurial plan should be as detailed and clear as possible. Someone should be able to read it, even a bank or investor, and have clear vision of what you are striving to establish in the earth, and be able to examine whether it is a vision they desire to invest in. This is the reason God told Habakkuk to write the vision and make it plain.

<u>Write</u> in the Hebrew is *kathab* **and means:**
1. to write, record, enroll
2. to inscribe, engrave, write in, write on
3. to write down, describe in writing
4. register, to decree
5. to be written, to be written down, be recorded, be enrolled

Habakkuk engraved the vision by writing it upon the tables so those who ran to it would be impacted by it. By doing this, Habakkuk was planting and establishing the vision in the earth and making sure everyone that was a part of it had revelation of it.

Engraving is like a tattoo deeply carved into something. It does not change because it is carved in. It hurts, can bleed and requires pressure because of the depth needed to make the imprint.

When you are making the vision plain, you are doing a prophetic activation that sets an established eternal foundation for what you are going to walk out through your faith.

As you search out the questions in this chapter, jot down what comes to your thoughts and examine your entrepreneurial vision before the Lord. Then use your answers to form a standard vision plan that will be at the end of this chapter.

What is the entrepreneurial vision of market place ministry that God has given you?

_____
_____
_____
_____
_____
_____
_____
_____
_____
_____

What is the purpose of the entrepreneurial vision, book, etc.?

What are your product/s within the vision?

Who is your audience? Who will benefit from your product and/or vision?

What reasons are they your audience and how will they benefit?

What makes your product and/or vision different than your competitors? (seek revelation & journal on this from a spiritual and natural point of view)?

What is your missions statement?

What is the scriptural foundation for your book, vision, etc.?

What is God striving to establish in the earth through your marketplace vision?

What location and region does God want you to plant your vision?

How is the location and region essential to your product and the work God desires you to do?

USE THE FOLLOWING FORMAT TO CREATE YOUR VISION PLAIN

I encourage you to type this plan as it is what banks, grant corporations, and investors will want to review as they consider connecting and investing in your vision.

- VISION TITLE
- VISION PURPOSE
- SCRIPTURE FOUNDATION & EXPLANATION FOR THE VISION
- MISSION STATEMENT
- FOUNDER'S INFORMATION
- CONTACT INFORMATION (Website, Email Address, Telephone Number, Street Address, Facebook, Twitter, Instagram, Blogging, LinkedIn info, etc.)
- ENTREPRENEUR SERVICES RENDERED (If there are multiple compartments of the vision, list them all in bullet point form and then answer the following questions under each compartment).
  - What will the ministry/business/organization be doing?
  - How will the ministry/business/organization go about fulfilling its vision?
  - What population will you be serving & what reasons you chose this population?
  - What makes your ministry/business/product unique from similar vision carriers?

- o What makes the ministry/business/organization unique from its competitors?
- o How often will this service occur?
- o What region or sphere of influence will this vision occur in?
- o What reasons this region or sphere of influence is essential to your vision?
- ENTREPRENEUR GUIDELINES:
  - o GUIDELINES AND REGULATIONS FOR THE MINISTRY/ORGANIZATION/BUSINESS
  - o GUIDELINES FOR THOSE YOU WILL BE SERVING
  - o GUIDELINES FOR THOSE WHO WILL BE WORKING IN THE MINISTRY/ORGANIZATION/BUSINESS (what accountabilities and personal responsibilities do you need to put in place to keep the ministry in alignment with what God is requiring you to fulfill within the ministry?)

_____
_____
_____
_____
_____
_____
_____
_____
_____
_____
_____
_____
_____
_____
_____
_____
_____
_____
_____
_____
_____
_____
_____
_____
_____
_____
_____

SHORT & LONG-TERM VISION PLAN

After you write your entrepreneurial vision, it is important to create short and long-term plans to help you successfully bring the vision to pass. You can have a broad entrepreneurial plan that requires years to achieve, and that even generations ahead will have to fulfill. You can also have a short-term ministry plan that will enable you to work on your broad ministry plan without becoming burnt-out, or releasing and doing things out of the timing of the Lord.

Your short-term plan can be for a year, two years, five years, etc. The Lord will lead you in what is realistic and obtainable for you. I have a broad vision plan of all God desires me to fulfill. It is impossible to think I can plant, plow, and build each part of my vision at the same time. I therefore, seek God for what I am to work on in my current season of life. Sometimes, I am working on a couple or multiple areas at a time. But God releases them where the work is overlapping, and where they build on top of one another. I usually consistently work on my short-term vision for a year -January through November. In November of each year, I take a sabbatical and examine, re-evaluate, add, and take away from the plan as I prepare for the next year. My sabbatical is included in my plan, so I can rest while continuing to complete any last-minute tasks related to my plan. This enables me to keep balanced in all God has granted to my hands, and not get overburdened by my life's vision and destiny. Remember destiny is a lifestyle walk with God. It is not a destination but a journey. You have destiny moments of success in your journey, but will be towering with God throughout your life with him.

An Example Of A Long-term Vision Plan:

- Plant a church
- Open a shelter for homeless women
- Write a book on healing the abused woman

An Example Of A Short-term Vision Plan:

January 2017-November 2017

- Seek God for a leadership team
- Begin having church services in my home twice a month
- Set up trainings for my team in leadership, eldership, evangelism
- Have weekly 5am prayer via conference call with my team every Saturday
- Have weekly bible study via conference call with my team every Thursday at 8pm
- Meet with each team member monthly for a mentoring session and to build them up in their personal walk with Jesus, and personal gifts and calling
- Explore information on how to open a shelter
- Volunteer at a women's shelter twice a month to learn the dynamics of operating a shelter

- Write vision, missions statement, policies and procedures, and laws for the shelter
- Explore grants and funding for women's shelters. Narrow down at least three grants that are in line with our vision. Have a clear understanding of their operations so I can begin writing on the grant and funding requirements in January 2018
- Spend time before the Lord on Wednesday and Friday from 12pm to 2pm writing a book. Be okay if God does not give you anything. There is an anointing to scribe that will come upon you and even wake you up to write, or draw you away to scribe. If God is not leading you to write in your scheduled time, use it to do research on your book topic; also use it to cleanse any unhealed areas in you or challenges that is blocking the scribe anointing on your life; use it to just be before the Lord and rest while he downloads revelation into your spirit. When it is time for you to begin scribing, he will awaken it in you, and unction you to write. **Psalms 45:1** *My heart is inditing a good matter: I speak of the things which I have made touching the king: my tongue is the pen of a ready writer.* **The Message Bible** *My heart bursts its banks, spilling beauty and goodness. I pour it out in a poem to the king, shaping the river into words. Inditing* means "to gush, flow, to stir." It is an anointing that overtakes you and you begin to spill out the heart of God through words.
- Take a sabbatical in November to reevaluate, reflect, revive, refresh, and plan for next year.

Spend time seeking God for your short-term and long-term entrepreneurial vision plan. Use the example above to engrave your plan in the earth.

Long-term Vision Plan:

Short-term Vision Plan:

CHARACTER OF AN ENTREPRENEURIAL VISION CARRIER

1. Integral
2. Possess the mind, character & nature of God
3. Possess Godly vision & can convey that vision to others
4. Prayer warriors, studiers & doers of God's Word
5. Lifestyle of fasting & consecration
6. Enthusiastic, & passionate about themselves, life, destiny & the vision
7. Honors their covenant relationship with God
8. Motivated in their ordained purpose - sold out to God & purpose
9. Self-confident
10. Believe in themselves, their potential & the vision
11. Self-encouragers & self-motivators
12. Focused
13. Prophetic & future minded
14. Risk takers
15. Go getters - go after what they desire
16. Bounce back quickly from mishaps, failures & challenges
17. Intelligent
18. Wise
19. Emotionally balanced
20. Can handle and pursue constructive criticism
21. Creative
22. Inventive
23. Persuasive in drawing their remnant to their endeavors
24. Consistent in plowing the vision & plowing destiny
25. Rigid with not compromising God's destiny & vision for their lives
26. Adaptable, versatile & flexible with allowing him to change it when needed or with how it is to unfold in the earth
27. Understand their worth & value while lacking compromise
28. Multitaskers
29. Resourceful
30. Willing to do the work of the vision behind the scenes and in the forefront
31. Effective in setting up internal structures to build a foundation for the vision
32. Disciplined & Dedicated
33. A laborer - hard workers eager to work the vision with fervency and persistence
34. Decisive, good decision makers & quick thinkers that trust that they carry the mind & vision of God
35. Learners and knowers of their product, field, & clientele
36. Fervent in seizing every moment & opportunity to siege destiny & to advance their entrepreneurial plan
37. Integral & strong money management skills
38. Financial investors in their destiny, entrepreneurial vision, & their future
39. Generational minded & make decisions based on investing in future generations
40. Effective planners & sticklers to goals

41. Friendly, team oriented, & willing to take risk to connect with the right people to advance in destiny & their entrepreneurial vision
42. A heart for people & souls
43. Celebrators & encouragers of the success of others
44. Teachable
45. Accountable to God, mentors, destiny & the vision
46. Life learners
47. Willing to reassess self, goals, destiny, decisions, & the vision & make changes as God directs
48. Pursuers of continual success & advancement
49. Rewarders of themselves & others when they do well
50. Praise & worshippers who give God the glory for successful destiny vision carrier moments

Which characteristics are your greatest strengths?

Which characteristics do you need to improve on and why?

_____
_____
_____
_____
_____
_____
_____
_____
_____
_____
_____
_____
_____
_____
_____
_____
_____
_____
_____
_____
_____
_____
_____
_____
_____

Journal at least three goals you can commit to in order to improve in areas of character weakness.

_____
_____
_____
_____
_____
_____
_____
_____
_____
_____

NUGGETS FOR LAUNCHING MARKETPLACE ENDEAVORS

It requires finances to launch your entrepreneurial vision. God will fund the vision, but he will also require you to sow into what he has granted to your hands. I recommend saving at least $1000 to $2000 so you can pay the initial fees to launch your vision. Use the following steps to establish your entrepreneurial vision in the earth. These nuggets can be a lot of work and can even be frustrating at times. If they become too frustrating or you do not have time, **DO NOT QUIT OR PUT THESE ENDEAVORS OFF FOR LATER**! Pay someone to complete the endeavors for you. I listed some service providers. There are a host of others that you can consult with as well. I paid someone to assist me and it was a weight off my shoulders. Whether you do them or someone else, get them done. **DO NOT LAUNCH YOUR VISION WITHOUT THESE BASICS.** You can risk getting into fraud and be robbing of the goods, services, etc., that you release into the earth. You want your entrepreneurial business launched through the integrity and character of God. These basic nuggets will assist you in making sure you are in line with God and the law.

Launching Your Market Place Ministry

- ✓ First decide if you want to be a 501C3, sole proprietor, a corporation or a LLC which is a Limited Liability Company. This determines how your taxes are filed and how the government views your market place endeavor. The IRS has information that can help you determine which status is best for you. You have to choose one status. You can switch at any time, but you will have refiling fees. After you decide this, go to the IRS website to be incorporated in one of these areas. IRS.Gov
- ✓ If you decide to be 501C3 please know there is a whole other list of forms you will have to complete and fees you will have to pay. IRS.Gov will have this information on their website.
- ✓ After you apply for your status, learn when you need to submit your taxes and place this on your calendar, so you can submit them when they are due. An accountant or a tax agent can help you file your taxes.
- ✓ As you are making money, you need to keep a percentage to cover the taxes you will need to pay. You should safely withhold 25% to 30% of your earnings to cover taxes. 501C3 does not pay taxes, unless there is fraud, or the government requires it, but the other status pays taxes. This may change in the future. I, therefore recommend the other statuses over 501C3.
- ✓ Purchase a file cabinet where you can keep all receipts and donation information, so you can have this information for your taxes.
- ✓ Apply for EIN number from your State. Which is your employer identification number. You need this number whether you are a church, business, or organization. Every state has their own rules and website, so you need to google this information and apply.
- ✓ After you acquire the IRS status and EIN, use this information to open a bank account in the name of your market place ministry.
- ✓ Open a PayPal account in your market place ministry name. Apply for a PayPal Here device. Or you can open a Square account and apply for a Square device.

Check the percentage rates that tells how much they receive and you receive from donations and goods and then determine which service is best for you. Both of these services have apps that can downloaded to your phone, computers, tablets. This allows you to receive, sale, and take donations from basically anywhere in the world or from wherever you are.
- ✓ I highly recommend creating a website to promote your market place ministry. Use Search Engine Optimization (SEO) analytics and Google analytics to make your website more viewable where people can find you. Google SEO analytics and Google Analytics to learn more about how they work.
- ✓ I highly recommend creating a Facebook, Twitter, Instagram and/or LinkedIn account to further market your ministry.
- ✓ Google the Small Business Administration as they tend to have funds, services, and workshops for entrepreneurs.
- ✓ The department of human services can provide information regarding taking insurance payments and Medicaid payments. You can also google this information.
- ✓ There are also grant websites you can research as you can receiving governmental assistance to help fund some of your entrepreneurial endeavors. Be mindful that some grants have clauses that may be contrary to your spiritual beliefs. You do not want to compromise the vision and standards God gives you for money, so avoid funding of this nature.
- ✓ Begin researching marketing tactics that best suits your brand. Implement them consistently to see progress and success regarding your entrepreneurial vision.

Book Publishing
- ✓ Write the book.
- ✓ Ask God for a vision for your book cover.
- ✓ While writing, seek someone to complete your book cover.
- ✓ Seek someone to edit and format your book.
- ✓ Simultaneously, you will want to acquire a ISBN number and copyright.
- ✓ Copyright can be attained online at https://www.copyright.gov.
- ✓ ISBN number can be obtained at https://www.myidentifiers.com. If you want to do a paperback and hardcopy for your book, then you need to acquire two ISBN's for the same book. If you are doing an eBook on Amazon, you do not need another ISBN number. But other places will require you to have a ISBN number for your eBook as well as the paperback and/or hardback book.
- ✓ You can seek a publisher, or you can use Amazon to self-publish your book. You can do Amazon or CreateSpace to Amazon. Percentages and processes for each of these publishing choices are different.
- ✓ Follow the prompts on Amazon or CreateSpace to self-publish your book.

If you desire further assistance in this area, I highly recommend Amanda Barnhill of Euodoo Enterprises. She is a business strategist skilled in helping people build the internal structure of their entrepreneurial vision, so that as they release it in the earth, sustainable progress and success will be their portion.

Her website is http://www.euodooenterprisesllc.com
Her email address is Euodooenterprises12@gmail.com
Amanda Barnhill also provides administrative services for editing self-publishing books. Contact her if you desire to pay someone to complete this service for you rather than doing it yourself.

I recommend the following artist for book covers:
- Tasha Hyatt & Tashema Davis for cover pictures
- Reenita Keys for putting your book cover together

To encourage you during this time of working on your entrepreneurial vision, I encourage you to purchase the audible book "*Soar! Build Your Vision From The Ground Up,*" by *T.D. Jakes*. Listen to it over and over. I have slept to this book and it empowered me tremendously understanding the challenges and successes of launching a vision.

Begin fervently working on these nuggets. DO NOT LAX OR SLACK! Seek accountability from your tribe so you can remain consistent. Pay someone to assist you with completing the tasks if necessary! SHIFT!

Share your thoughts as you read these nuggets. Journal your thoughts whether good or bad. Deal with any negative thoughts in prayer with God. Journal any encouragement or strategies he gives you.

_____
_____
_____
_____
_____
_____
_____
_____
_____
_____
_____
_____
_____
_____
_____

Journal what you can sacrifice in your personal life to produce finances that can help fund your vision? (What spending habits can you cut back on to increase your cash flow investment into the vision? E.g. going to the hairdresser once a month instead of twice a month, doing your own manicures and pedicures, taking a lunch rather than eating out, eating out twice a month instead of every other day). How can you begin saving to invest in your entrepreneurial vision? Seek God as to whether asking people to sow into your endeavors is sufficient. If he says "yes," write a letter to them sharing the vision. Meet with them, share the vision, and then give them the letter so they can further consider your offer. Give them a timeline for sowing. Thank them whether they sow or not as they may sow in the future.

Complete a google search and compare your vision to others that are similar. Journal keys and strategies that made their vision successful, and seek God as to whether they will be beneficial in your vision endeavor. Implement them as he leads.

Google similar marketplace endeavors. Examine what they have purchased and invested in to make their vision successful. Write a detailed business financial plan (even down to how much a chair for your office will cost; be detailed) of your NEEDS to make your vision successful. This is important as though you will be relying on God to fund the vision, you will have to invest in the vision and know how much it will cost to bring it to pass. Then make a separate list of what you NEED RIGHT NOW to make your business successful, then begin working on obtaining those items. Be okay with having nice used items, donations, etc. You can acquire nicer items once your vision is established and flourishing.

> ***Luke 14:27-28*** *And whosoever doth not bear his cross, and come after me, cannot be my disciple. For which of you, intending to build a tower, sitteth not down first, and counteth the cost*

NUGGETS FOR SOCIAL MEDIA ADVERTISING

- ✓ As an entrepreneur, we must treat social media like it is a part of our vision and make it a job duty. It is not social media, but an avenue for transforming and SHIFTING people's lives.
- ✓ Because of the way social media is set up, we must understand that the same people are not looking at our statuses all the time. The statuses are set up to reach random people. Though we may think we are bombarding the same people with our post, we are not doing that. Though people may not respond to our post, that does not necessarily mean that they do not like what we are sharing, tired of it, or it is not reaching them. Do not let assumptions and perceived inadequacies dictate you following through with your job tasks on social media.
- ✓ People do not know you are an expert in something if you do not say anything. You must post if you want to use social media for ministry and business.
- ✓ Be consistent with posting about your ministry, business, book, events, etc., at least once a day.
- ✓ Use these options to share about your business:
  - What reasons is your business, ministry, event, book, important?
  - Share personal and client testimonies and breakthroughs
  - Building credibility on social media is about consistency of message. Search God for what your unique message is, quest, purpose is, and say it until everyone is saying that is your unique message. For example my unique message is to SHIFT people, regions, and spheres into the likeness of God and his kingdom. I hashtag SHIFT so much until people equate SHIFT with anything that I post – with who I am.
  - Have others share your posts. Ask specific friends and team members to be conscious to push your post. Ask them if you can post on their wall, that way they can share your post when they see it on their page.
  - Share things people want and/or need to hear as this builds them up and builds your friends list.
  - Share fun stuff and be friendly to draw people to your character and then they will be drawn to your ministry or business.
  - Talk to people on your posts and other posts, so they can have conversations rather than just like or give one word responses.
  - Get involved in discussions and engage people on other posts, so you can draw people to you.
  - Find articles on different topics related to what is important to you, your ministry, business, event, etc., and use some of the information in your postings.
  - Translate information in a manner that is more empowering or proclaiming the gospel or marketing your business that is not preachy and religious. For example my key theme is #SHIFT:
    - Why is SHIFTING important
    - Deal with fears in SHIFTING
    - Share keys to SHIFTING
    - Teach people how to SHIFT
    - Deal with the trials and blessings of SHIFTING

- Identify and draw Kingdom SHIFTERS to you
✓ Your ideal clients or ministry connections are like you. Cultivate what resonates with your tribe – the people who are like you and who you want to be connected to.
✓ Make statuses where you are just posting one sentence statements or questions.
✓ Create statuses that share key and unique wisdom.
✓ Take advantage of live videos to build relationships with your audience and draw people to your page.
✓ Place your live videos on Youtube so you can post them to your page in the future and so people can have access to your wisdom, ministry and business endeavors.
✓ Be cognizant of how you represent yourself and God on social media. Do not post, respond to, or engage in any conversations that do not edify God and that makes you look suspect in your character and integrity.
✓ In addition to your personal page, consider setting up a business or ministry page. On facebook, you can also set up group pages to discuss topics related to your books, business or ministry endeavors or passions. You are able to schedule post days in advance on business and ministry pages. This is great if you want to set aside a time to schedule your posts for the week and as they post to your entrepreneurial pages, you can repost them to your personal page and to other social media sites.
✓ Be open to learning and exploring social media, until you cultivate an atmosphere that is conducive to who you are and who you desire to be.

List at least three weekly social media goals you can commit to. Be realistic and consistent in your endeavors.

_____
_____
_____
_____
_____
_____
_____
_____
_____
_____
_____
_____
_____
_____
_____
_____
_____
_____
_____
_____

DESPISE NOT SMALL BEGINNINGS

Proverbs 20:21 *An inheritance may be gotten hastily at the beginning; but the end thereof shall not be blessed.*

Zechariah 4:9-10 *The hands of Zerubbabel have laid the foundation of this house; his hands shall also finish it; and thou shalt know that the Lord of hosts hath sent me unto you. For who hath despised the day of small things? for they shall rejoice, and shall see the plummet in the hand of Zerubbabel with those seven; they are the eyes of the Lord, which run to and fro through the whole earth.*

Despise is *buz* in the Hebrew and means, "to disrespect, to despise, hold in contempt, hold as insignificant, show despite toward."

The Amplified Bible *The hands of Zerubbabel have laid the foundations of this house; his hands shall also finish it. Then you shall know (recognize and understand) that the Lord of hosts has sent me [His messenger] to you. Who [with reason] despises the day of small things? For these seven shall rejoice when they see the plummet in the hand of Zerubbabel. [These seven] are the eyes of the Lord which run to and fro throughout the whole earth.*

Haggai 2:3-9 The Message Bible *Is there anyone here who saw the Temple the way it used to be, all glorious? And what do you see now? Not much, right? So get to work, Zerubbabel!' – God is speaking. Get to work, Joshua son of Jehozadak – high priest!' Get to work, all you people!' – God is speaking.*

Yes, get to work! For I am with you.' The God-of-the-Angel-Armies is speaking! 'Put into action the word I covenanted with you when you left Egypt. I'm living and breathing among you right now. Don't be timid. Don't hold back.' "This is what God-of-the-Angel-Armies said: 'Before you know it, I will shake up sky and earth, ocean and fields. And I'll shake down all the godless nations. They'll bring bushels of wealth and I will fill this Temple with splendor.' God-of-the-Angel-Armies says so. 'I own the silver, I own the gold.' Decree of God-of-the-Angel-Armies. This Temple is going to end up far better than it started out, a glorious beginning but an even more glorious finish: a place in which I will hand out wholeness and holiness.' Decree of God-of-the-Angel-Armies."

God has a strategic plan for how you are to build his vision. He knows what it takes to keep it grounded, healthy, solid, fortified, and protected. Though your vision may be similar to others, and you can glean from them, there is always a specific strategy and pattern for bringing your blueprint to pass. There is always something unique and tailor made to you and the vision you are carrying that will be distinct and that will require you to truly hear and walk with God to birth and establish your vision in the earth. What may seem easy for others may not be easy for you and vice versa. Actually, we never know what price people are paying behind the scenes to bring their God ordained visions to pass. Sometimes, what you are enduring as a vision carrier is a sign to others in some fashion. Ezekiel carried many visions and blueprints of the Lord and many of them were warnings unto the House of Israel.

Ezekiel 4:1-3 "*Now you son of man, get yourself a brick, place it before you and inscribe a city on it, Jerusalem. "Then lay siege against it, build a siege wall, raise up a ramp, pitch camps and place battering rams against it all around. "Then get yourself an iron plate and set it up as an iron wall between you and the city, and set your face toward it so that it is under siege, and besiege it. This is a sign to the house of Israel.*

That word *sign* means *ot* in the Hebrew and means:
1. sign, signal, distinguishing mark, ensign (badge of office or authority)
2. banner (banners represent the kingdom they are a part of),
3. beacon (a person or thing that illuminates or inspires), token (badge or demonstration)
4. prodigy (marvelous example - extraordinary talent or ability
5. remembrance which is a memorial
6. miracle, standard, warning
7. proof, (that God is God - that God is with you)

Your pathway is speaking volumes and may be the red flag that those who are cutting corners, microwaving their blueprint, prostituting their vision, are secretly struggling or discouraged in their vision and need to be pricked to reorder themselves with God.

What you are comparing yourself to may not even be of God or the fullness of God. You may also be the sign the world needs as a standard of the true blue print and workings of God.

It is also important to embrace who you are as a trailblazer and pioneer of God's unique blue print. Ezekiel says set your face towards it so that it is under siege.

The only way you can really tower as a vision carrier is to face it head on. This allows you to lay hold of it, such that you become it and can be fortified inside of it.

You cannot just do the work while not fully embracing it. The more you reject it or waver with embracing it, the more it opens the door to unnecessary warfare, and to the enemy having access to siege it.

You also risk becoming a sign that is flaky rather than solidified in God. Lay siege and besiege it. Become it! #SHIFT

Do not despise what God is doing right now. Remain faithful and continue to set a solid foundation. You are doing everything you are supposed to be doing. Continue to remain faithful and do it as I am leading you. Do the work in excellence and remain grounded in the vision. All else - the people, helpers, etc., will be added in due time.

When needed spend time meditating on the scriptures to encourage yourself in remaining fervent, focused, and empowered with working your entrepreneurial vision.

DECLARATION OF INDEPENDENCE

This chapter is inspired by my overseer, Apostle Jackie Green's, *"Spurned Into Apostleship Workbook."* After writing my declaration of independence from her workbook, I update it occasionally, and verbally decree it out loud to assert authority in towering destiny and regarding vision plans. My declaration of independence also fortifies me in towering over curses, strongholds, demons, wickedness, and anything else that attempts to hinder, alter, or destroy my destiny and Godly vision.

> *It is important that we understand the "power of declaration" when coming into our purpose and destiny. You must declare to principalities, power structures and people who you are.*
>
> *To declare according to Webster's dictionary means to "make known, state clearly, to announce officially or proclaim; to reveal, to indicate; to proclaim oneself to assert or affirm making something openly known; to make known in the face of contradictions and opposition, to state boldly."*
>
> *People can affirm you and encourage you, but you must make a declaration with your life, with your words, and with your actions. When these three align, there is going to be a profound release upon your life and in the lives of others.*

---

1. The Bible says: "Thou shall also decree a thing, and it shall be established unto thee; and the light shall shine upon you." Job 22:28 What does that verse mean to you? Read that verse in several other Bible versions for greater clarity.

    _____
    _____
    _____
    _____
    _____
    _____
    _____
    _____
    _____
    _____
    _____
    _____
    _____
    _____
    _____
    _____
    _____

2. Write a declaration using the information in the destiny chapters regarding what your talents, gifts, calling, and destiny is.)

I declare that I am called to:

_____
_____
_____
_____
_____
_____
_____
_____
_____
_____
_____
_____
_____
_____
_____
_____
_____

I declare that I am talented at?

_____
_____
_____
_____
_____
_____
_____
_____
_____
_____
_____
_____
_____
_____

I declare that I am gifted by the Holy Spirit in the areas of:

3. *I decree the spirit of God operating upon my life according to Isaiah 11:2 are:*

4. I decree I am called to:

_____

5. *I declare that enough is enough and the devil can no longer (list seven things the devil can no longer do in your life:*

_____

6. *I declare and decree according to Psalms 139 that I am fearfully and wonderfully made. I will not speak negative declarations about myself, ministry, vision, etc. I break every negative declaration about my (example: finances, body, health, future, ministry etc.). Spend time allowing God to show you negative decrees that need to be broken. Be specific in journaling the curses you need to break.*

_____
_____
_____
_____
_____
_____
_____
_____
_____
_____
_____
_____
_____
_____
_____
_____
_____
_____
_____
_____
_____

7. *I break all decrees, declarations and negative prophecies spoken over me by (list the people, parents, relatives, enemies, ex-spouses, co-workers or ministries etc.): Take your time and write out each decree regarding each person who has spoken negatively over your life*

_____
_____
_____
_____
_____
_____
_____
_____
_____
_____
_____
_____
_____
_____

8. *What is bothering you right now about your life, family, ministry or business? Journal and write a new decree to counter attack these thoughts and feelings. I recommend you type it out later and declare it regularly. If you are a Pastor or senior leader, you need to consider writing a declaration over your ministry or church. If you are a business owner or entrepreneur, consider writing a declaration over your business, organization, or entrepreneurial endeavor. If you have children, write a declaration and decree over their lives and future. If you are sick and dealing with infirmity, write scriptural decrees over your life. As you write the vision, decree it, it will be made plain in your life, destiny, and personal and entrepreneurial vision*

_____
_____
_____
_____
_____
_____
_____
_____
_____
_____
_____
_____
_____
_____
_____
_____
_____
_____
_____
_____
_____
_____
_____
_____
_____
_____
_____
_____
_____
_____

OBEDIENCE TO THE VISION

Obedience to God is key to journeying successfully in destiny and releasing your entrepreneurial vision in the earth. Obedience is a choice and a sacrifice. It requires faith and self-discipline to be obedient. You have to love the things God loves and hate the things that God hates. You have to desire God's will and purpose for your life, above what you think your purpose is or who and what others believe you should be. Your obedience will constantly be tested. You have to maintain a lifestyle of prayer, studying and living the word of God, and fasting, to sustain in obedience.

The word *obey* in the Hebrew is *sama* and means:
1. to hear intelligently (often with implication of attention, obedience, etc.; causatively, to tell, etc.)
2. attentively, call (gather) together, carefully, certainly, consent, consider, be content, declare, diligently, discern, give ear, discern
3. to hear (perceive by ear) to hear of or concerning
4. to hear (have power to hear) to hear with attention or interest, listen to
5. to understand (language), to hear (of judicial cases), to listen, give heed
6. to consent, agree to, grant request to, listen to, yield to, to obey, be obedient

Basically obey means to hear God clearly and do what He says.

- Good ideas and good people will come for your obedience.
- Appealing desires and lustful attractions will come for your obedience.
- Need fillers that cause you to sacrifice yourself, your character, the vision, or your progress will come your obedience.
- Quick fixes and easy but altered pathways will come for your obedience.
- Fear, panic and worry will come for your obedience.
- False glory and famed glory will come for your obedience.
- The enemy will always be after your obedience.

At times, you will experience mental and psychological warfare as you contend to remain grounded in the Lord. Sometimes this war ceases when you choose the will of God and rest in his peace. Sometimes it escalates because the enemy is enraged by your decision, so he increases his attack against you. I would say the greatest defense you have against the enemy regarding obedience is knowing your identity in Christ. The world would say that identity was being one's authentic self. I define healthy identity as being who God created us to be. Biblically, identity means being created in the likeness and image of God as *identity* began in the garden with Adam and Eve.

> ***Genesis 1:26*** *And God said, Let us make man in our image, after our likeness: and let them have dominion over the fish of the sea, and over the fowl of the air, and over the cattle, and over all the earth, and over every creeping thing that creepeth upon the earth.*

The Message Bible *God spoke: "Let us make human beings in our image, make them reflecting our nature So they can be responsible for the fish in the sea, the birds in the air, the cattle, And, yes, Earth itself, and every animal that moves on the face of Earth."*

Image is *selem* in the Hebrew and means:
1. to shade; a phantom, i.e. (figuratively) illusion
2. resemblance; hence, a representative figure, especially an idol
3. image, vain shew

Likeness in the Hebrew is *dmut* and means:
1. resemblance; concretely, model, shape; adverbially, like
2. fashion, like (-ness, as), manner, similitude

Dictionary.com defines of *likeness* as:
1. a representation, picture, or image, especially a portrait
2. the state or fact of being like
3. the semblance or appearance of something; guise
4. correspondence in appearance; something that corresponds
5. Synonyms: affinity, agreement, alikeness, analogousness, analogy, appearance, carbon, clone, comparableness, comparison, conformity, copy, counterpart, dead ringer, delineation, depiction, ditto, double, effigy, equality, equivalence, facsimile, form, guise, identicalness, identity, image, knock-off, lookalike, model, parallelism, photocopy, photograph, picture, portrait, replica, representation, reproduction, resemblance, sameness, semblance, similarity, simile, similitude, study, uniformity, Xerox

Dictionary.com defines *identity* as:
1. the state or fact of remaining the same one or ones, as under varying aspects or conditions
2. the condition of being oneself or itself, and not another
3. condition or character as to who a person or what a thing is
4. the state or fact of being the same one as described
5. the sense of self, providing sameness and continuity in personality over time and sometimes disturbed in mental illnesses, as schizophrenia
6. exact likeness in nature or qualities
7. an instance or point of sameness or likeness

A healthy identity is birthed through relationship with God. We have a healthy identity when we understand:

- ✓ Who God is and is not (our creator and ruler)
- ✓ Who we are and are not (our identity and purpose)
- ✓ That we are a unique Xerox copy of God and are made in his image, therefore we have his capabilities and authorities in us
- ✓ Can actively live in our authentic self, based on who God is and who we are through God (our destiny and generational inheritance through him)

When we are clear in our identity and do not desire to be or engage in anything that does not represent God, we possess the power to defeat disobedience. It is important to recognize when our identity is being challenged, needs strengthened, or needs to mature to tower in the current dimension we are journeying in regarding destiny and progressing in our entrepreneurial vision. These times will come, but identifying them quickly and building ourselves up in the truth of God is key to not yielding to disobedience. When we have nothing to prove, when we are not trying to get our needs and desires met outside of God's will, when we can celebrate our successes and progresses and not covet someone else's, when we are comfortable with the vision and blueprint God has given us for destiny and the entrepreneurial vision, we can annihilate disobedience.

Self-care is essential to maintaining a healthy identity. Deliverance and healing has to be your daily bread. You have to want to be who God desires you to be and pursue it as a part of your daily lifestyle. Reaching out to your covering and mentors when you need breakthrough and cannot acquire it in personal prayer. Remaining accountable to the goals needed to breakthrough to deliverance and healing is essential to self-care, and maintaining a healthy identity. Do not allow the enemy to isolate or shame you into thinking that pursuing deliverance and healing is bad thing. That if you were really walking in destiny and were a good vision carrier, you would not have struggles. It is a lie from the pit of hell. Even Jesus needed the angels to come and encourage him in the garden of Gethsemane as he walked out his destiny lifestyle as savior (*Luke 22*). Many in the bible that yielded to disobedience were not secure in who they were in God, were not secure in who God was in them, were lusting or yielding to the flesh, were isolated and alone, and were bound by the enemy. When you embrace deliverance and healing as a lifestyle, you are quick to take the necessary steps to have your identity restored in the wellness and truth of God.

What did you learn from this chapter?

What areas do you need to improve on regarding being obedient to God?

How would you know if you were bound by a demonic stronghold? Journal in detail.

What would you do if you were bound by a demonic stronghold? Journal in detail.

_____
_____
_____
_____
_____
_____
_____
_____
_____
_____
_____
_____
_____
_____
_____
_____
_____
_____
_____

What is a healthy identity?

_____
_____
_____
_____
_____
_____
_____
_____
_____
_____
_____
_____
_____
_____
_____
_____

Journal what your healthy identity looks like?

Journal how you know when your identity is unhealthy?

Journal a step by step vision plan you can put in place to help you restore or mature your identity?

YOUR ACCOUNTABILITY TRIBE

The Familiar Versus The Chosen

Often when we become stoked about walking in our destiny and releasing our entrepreneurial vision in the earth, we immediately begin telling those close to us and expecting them to support our vision. Though our families and friends love us dearly and want the best for us, often they are not the persons to be a part of our endeavors, or even to glean from our endeavors. And though not always the case, much of the time, our family and loved ones do not really connect or invest in what we are doing until much later when we have shown some sustaining success and have become a sufficient testimony of destiny attainment. NOW THAT YOU KNOW THIS, PLEASE STOP TAKING THEIR LACK OF SUPPORT OR INVESTMENT PERSONAL. IT IS NOT PERSONAL! GOD PROVIDES THE TRIBE!

- ✓ Often who you think should automatically support and help you are not WHO GOD CHOSE for you and your vision.
- ✓ Many close to you are too familiar to be accountable to destiny and your entrepreneurial vision in the manner you need in order to maintain stability and momentum in what God has called you too. Familiarity tends to breed laziness, stagnation, and a tendency to put things off until tomorrow when God needs them done today.
- ✓ Sometimes God is doing a personal work in you, and after you have grown in destiny maturity and being able to adequately govern destiny and your entrepreneurial vision, he will allow those close to you to be a part of the vision. In this case, you will be sold out to the vision and not allow familiarity to sway you in your decisions concerning destiny or your entrepreneurial vision.
- ✓ Many close to you may be equipped to assist you, but are not called to the vision God has granted to your hands. You cannot assume that just because they can do something, they are the ones to help you. Many people have gifts and talents, but do they have integrity, character, balance, fortitude, stamina, perseverance, a good work ethic, spiritual maturity, etc.
- ✓ Does your family and loved ones possess the DNA of your vision and understand the voice and language of what God has granted to your hands? You cannot be so quick to fill positions, that you choose people that do not possess the ability to carry your entrepreneurial vision and do not have the fortitude to endure hard seasons. This is key because some seasons will be hard. If people are not there by God's design, they are more apt to opt out when the planting, plowing, building, and establishing gets hard. No matter how successful you are in destiny and in launching your entrepreneurial vision.
- ✓ Many close to you may not have God's heart for the region, spheres of influence, focal point, and population of people God has called you too. This is essential because they will speak against it and become betrayers, naysayers, distractors, discouragers, and curses of you and the entrepreneurial vision when they do not

have God's heart for who you are and what you are doing. They will tend to waver and want to implement plan "B" and may not have the faith to stick with God's plan. It is very difficult to build with someone who does not have the heart or faith for what you are doing. If God has strategically said someone is to help you, ask God to give them his heart and unwavering faith for the vision and for the eyes of their understanding to be enlightened concerning the vision. Know that your dedication and faithfulness is the best example and drawing they will have in connecting and aligning with what God has said. If you are fickle in your consistency to destiny and your entrepreneurial vision, then know that others will be fickle and distrustful of the vision.

God Chooses The Tribe

Sometimes you are called to equip and train your team and they grow up in the entrepreneurial vision with you. What they need to walk in destiny, while helping you to build has not been awakened in them yet, and part of your calling may be to stir it up, and help them release it in the earth. If God says this is your lot, DO NOT SHUN IT. There will be an acceleration anointing upon you and your team if you embrace it. Remember Jesus only had three years with the disciples and apostles, and they were and have been the most influential preachers, teachers, and miracle workers that we all glean from to this day. What God is granting to your hands may be multifaceted, generational, and expansive.

- ✓ You could be called to mentor, or be a spiritual mother and father to others.
- ✓ God could be using you to bridge generational gaps.
- ✓ There could be dimensions of you that need to be released in the earth and as you mentor, parent, and empower, others facets of you are also launched in the earth.
- ✓ God may not want tradition and religion intertwined in your entrepreneurial vision, so he sends you fresh hearts who are committed to hearing and doing the "now" work of his kingdom.
- ✓ Sometimes for what you are doing, it is easier to work with those who are not set in their beliefs and ways. God will send eager learners who can be molded in this mind and ways, who possess his heart to build and can be shaped into his character as they build. They will not be perfect, but most of them will be easily repentant, want to please God, want God to get glory, and have his spirit of excellence for their destiny and the entrepreneurial vision.

Jesus team consisted of those who had eager hearts, but required training and empowerment. They became a mighty force to be reckoned with. Ask God to reveal to you who your team is? Ask him to show you the reason he chose these persons and how they are to impact your destiny, the entrepreneurial vision, and who you are to impact their destiny and life's vision. Journal what he says. In his timing, approach them and ask them to pray about being a part of your team. Ask them to search God for their purpose in your life, as a team member, and how their destiny and life's vision is intertwined in the work God is asking them to be a part of. Give them a specific time to seek God then meet again and discuss what God has told each of you. If they are on board, go forth in creating a healthy team environment. If they are not, then respect what they state, and wait for God to release them or to bring someone else to take their place. Sometimes people will reject the work of the Lord. But this does not stop the work of the Lord. Do not take it personal. Respect their choice and move forward. God will honor you regardless and your destiny nor vision will not lack despite the choices of others.

God Protects The Vision

There is specific seasons of birthing, reaping, and harvest. All lack of fruit is not demonic. God will not allow seasons of fruit and harvest so that Babylon which is the world's system, religion or tradition, or the enemy cannot steal it.

You always hear the famous saying that "Everyone cannot go where you are going." Well if you are carrying a God ordained vision, it is a fact. God will separate you, so you can birth and advance the vision successfully and sufficiently. He will sterilize your spiritual environment, so you can birth in a dimension of life where your entrepreneurial vision will not be contaminated.

Sometimes this is the reason you have not gone forth, birthed, or advanced the vision. You think it is because you are not being recognized, the leader or people cannot value or see who you are, you are stuck, everyone is being blessed but you, or the devil is fighting your breakthrough to birth forth. But it is really because God refuse to let you birth in season or among people who will contaminate, stifle, dishonor, steal, or kill what he put in you. This is a love and gift not punishment. This is protection not delay. This is a blessing and favor not denial. Stop demanding people receive you and help you. Receive the protected love, grace, blessing and favor of God while asking him to SHIFT you out of kill zone into your birthing dimension. SHIFT!

Importance of Affiliate Covering, Mentoring, & Training

When I speak of affiliate covering for your entrepreneurial vision, I am not talking about someone who "Lord's" over you and your vision. But someone who you can partner with that has like or similar callings, has been where you are going or can see where you are going, has a heart for who you are in God and his kingdom, and can empower, guide, counsel, and hold you accountable to the personal and entrepreneurial vision he has given you. Affiliate covering is important because it provides:

- Accountability
- Correction
- Counsel
- Wisdom
- Guidance
- Confirmation
- Deliverance and healing of past and present wounds

- Keeps you doctrinally sound
- Keeps you God focused & submitted to God being the head of the vision, your calling, and your life
- Fortification, support, & prayer against warfare & life challenges
- Undergirding & hands on assistance with carrying, planting, plowing, & building your apostolic walk & ministry vision
- Training and equipping
- A safe place to learn, make mistakes, & grow
- An unconditional display of the love, grace, compassion, & refuge of God
- Fresh prophecy, insight, & enlightenment of vision
- Empowerment to consistently walk in your destiny vision
- Reintegration & confirmation of the work of the Lord, navigation of changes & SHIFTS necessary in your apostolic walk or ministry vision

Though your affiliate covering can mentor you and may be the main person covering your destiny and vision, it is okay to have other mentors and even affiliate coverings, as God will bring people who can help further empower, equip, and train you throughout your destiny and entrepreneurial journey. Mentors and even affiliate coverings can be seasonal or a lifetime. A mentor can also walk with you in different seasons and be absent in other seasons, while your main affiliate covering tends to be constant throughout every season. A person can have mentors and other affiliate coverings based on the needs, desires, skills and development he or she needs at that particular season of life. They generally provide wisdom, guidance, and instruction to someone that may be less experienced or just may need a safe place for self-examination, confirmation, support, empowerment, instruction and accountability. Though not always the case, they are usually older and wiser, and has personal experience or knowledge in the areas to which they are imparting. Life experiences can definitely be impacting as we can take keys that are shared and implement them in our lives, or we can use the wisdom to avoid life hardships and challenges. Moreover, shared commonality in experiences can serve as encouragement and empowerment to us overcoming life challenges. Mentors and extra covering can also provide additional protection and prayer for you, as you work on your goals and life endeavors.

I would say that your main affiliate covering is able to carry you in the spirit, carry your vision in the spirit, and help you to birth, plant, plow, build, and fully establish who you are and what you are doing in the earth. They value you and your vision as if it was their own and they feel as responsible for you being who God desires you to be and achieving all that he says as you do. Even to the point of encouraging you to acquire other covering, mentoring, training, and equipping when you need to further grow and advance in destiny and your entrepreneurial vision.

It is important to allow God to lead you in who your covering and mentors should be, and who you should receive training from.

- ✓ Connecting with someone who is popular or publicly platformed may not be best for you.
- ✓ Connecting with someone who has flowing gifts, but no character is surely not best for you. Character sustains a vision. If the person with bad character sinks, your ship sinks with them.
- ✓ Connecting with someone who is not available to you may not be best for you, especially if you are at the beginning stages of your destiny and/or with releasing your entrepreneurial vision. You need one on one covering and mentoring. Someone who can invest time into you and into your vision. As you mature, this is still necessary but does not have to be as frequent. Yet, you want to make sure you have the face and heart of those who are claiming to carry you and your vision in the spirit. They should be readily speaking into you, speaking into the vision, and encouraging you in the things of the Lord. Not just over the pulpit. Not just at a conference you attend. Not on social media. But face to face counsel, guidance, and training. Jesus had a daily relationship with his disciples and apostles. Think about that then search the Lord regarding the qualities of a healthy affiliate covering.

Ask God who is to be an affiliate covering of your ministry. Ask him to give you details regarding the person, ministry, business, etc., he chooses. Ask them to pray about covering you. Ask them to search the Lord for details concerning their role in your life and how they are to impact your destiny and entrepreneurial vision, then meet to collaborate on what God says. Make sure they are clear in who you are and what your life's vision is. Sometimes, they will have information about you that you may not have come into yet about yourself and the connection and vice versa. Be open to this. If it does not seem that they see you and your vision clearly, then it may not be the season for them to cover you or they may be a seasonal covering or mentor and not for a lifetime. Ask God for clarity and do as he leads. Your main covering will be revealed in his timing.

Accountability Partners

I always list accountability partners separate as YES coverings and mentors are accountability partners, we need healthy friends who can keep us accountable as well. Accountability partners are not people you tell your secrets and goals to, but you do listen to them when you need correcting in your thoughts, character, or actions. If you cannot respect the person enough to accept constructive feedback and criticism, then they are not your accountability partner. They are just acquaintances who lend you an ear when you are in crisis or are overburdened, yet your heart is to have agreement more than it is to change. If a person only agrees with you and helps to keep you bound to a victim mentality, they are not your accountability partner. Both of you have drama commonality but no true power within your connection to provide change in one another. Get accountability partners you can trust, respect, and be transformed with. SHIFT!

THE REGION KNOWS YOUR NAME

When we are releasing a vision in a particular region or area, we are actually building an altar for God's presence to be established.

> *Genesis 12:1-5 - Now the Lord had said unto Abram, Get thee out of thy country, and from thy kindred, and from thy father's house, unto a land that I will shew thee: And I will make of thee a great nation, and I will bless thee, and make thy name great; and thou shalt be a blessing: And I will bless them that bless thee, and curse him that curseth thee: and in thee shall all families of the earth be blessed. So Abram departed, as the Lord had spoken unto him; and Lot went with him: and Abram was seventy and five years old when he departed out of Haran.*
>
> *Verse 7 - And the Lord appeared unto Abram, and said, Unto thy seed will I give this land: and there builded he an altar unto the Lord, who appeared unto him.*

God knows where his presence needs to be established within the earth. It is important to be obedient to releasing the vision when and where he says and to seek him for the reason he has chosen a particular sphere of influence. It is also important to release the vision where God desires because God has instilled specific thoughts, revelation, and decrees into your region, and as you awaken what God has invested in the region regarding you, the region will begin to work with you to produce your destiny and vision in the earth.

> *Isaiah 49:1-4 Listen, O isles, unto me; and hearken, ye people, from afar; The Lord hath called me from the womb; from the bowels of my mother hath he made mention of my name. And he hath made my mouth like a sharp sword; in the shadow of his hand hath he hid me, and made me a polished shaft; in his quiver hath he hid me; And said unto me, Thou art my servant, O Israel, in whom I will be glorified. Then I said, I have laboured in vain, I have spent my strength for nought, and in vain: yet surely my judgment is with the Lord, and my work with my God.*
>
> *New Living Translation Listen to me, all you in distant lands! Pay attention, you who are far away! The Lord called me before my birth; from within the womb he called me by name. He made my words of judgment as sharp as a sword. He has hidden me in the shadow of his hand. I am like a sharp arrow in his quiver. He said to me, "You are my servant, Israel, and you will bring me glory." I replied, "But my work seems so useless! I have spent my strength for nothing and to no purpose. Yet I leave it all in the Lord's hand; I will trust God for my reward."*

We tend to think that being called means a plan has been set in our lives for the future, but *the Message Version* of this scripture reads:

The Message Version *Listen, far-flung islands, pay attention, faraway people: God put me to work from the day I was born. The moment I entered the world he named me.*

God put me and you to work from birth! We think destiny started when we became saved or when we begin doing something successful. It has been God's intentions that the call on our lives launched us into working for him from the day we left the womb.

The scripture says *"Listen, O isles, unto me; and hearken, ye people, from afar."* That word *isles* in the Hebrew means *region*. **Listen, O region!** That is a command or mandate proclamation. **Listen, O isles, O region!**

<u>Listen is šâma in the Hebrew and means:</u>
1. to hear intelligently and to be obedient
2. listen attentively, carefully, certainly
3. to consent, declare, discern, or give ear
4. to perceive, proclaim, publish, regard, report, to bear witness

The region has ears and you can command it to listen intelligently. You can command it to be diligently obedient to what you are saying, and to respond to what you are decreeing by mandating that it publishes your words, while bearing witness by producing the fruit of your words in the region. As you decree into the region, the region declares back to you what you said by producing your words in the land, people, businesses, ministries, organizations, atmosphere, climate, and heavenlies. Or in your specific case, by producing your words concerning your destiny and vision into the earth. These are words that God has already published in the region as the word *call* is *qârâ'* in the Hebrew and means, *"the idea of accosting a person." Accosting* means, *"to confront boldly, to approach especially with a greeting." Qara* also means, *"to call out to (i.e. properly, address by name, to call forth, cry (unto), (be) famous, guest, invite, mention, (give) name, preach, (make) proclamation, pronounce, publish.*

The region knows we are called from birth because God spoke our destiny into the ears of the region when we were in the womb. He did not just speak it, he cried it out with proclamation such that once we are born, the region can respond to our destiny as we begin to journey in life with God. As God gives you goals, plans, visions, strategies, and decrees to speak and complete in the region, you are awakening his will and purpose that was placed in the region at your birth. How awesome is that?

<u>Hearken is qâšab in the Hebrew and means:</u>
1. to prick up the ears, to incline, attend (of ears)
2. to give heed, regard, pay attention, listen, give attention

After you command the region to listen, you can prick the ears of (hearken) the people or your remnant, or those who will gleam from your destiny within the region and command them to listen, regard, attend, pay attention, give attention to you and to what the region is producing through you. As you lift up God through decrees, intercession, and warfare regarding what you speak in the region, God being exalted causes those who need who you are and what you are producing to be drawn to you. It is very important to cleanse out atmospheres about you and just in general, because whatever is spoken in that region the region listens, can hear it, and publishes that into its ground and sphere.

> ***Romans 8:19*** *declares "for the earnest expectation of the creature waiteth for the manifestation of the sons of God.*

The region is anxiously waiting on us, so it can manifest the depth of what God has put in it.

> ***English Standard Version*** *For we know that the whole creation has been groaning together in the pains of childbirth until now.*

We discern from this scripture that the region is a portal that constantly groans - constantly giving birth to our words, prayers, and declarations. The region is always in a birthing position. ***Genesis 1:28*** *declares "be fruitful and multiply."* This scripture is not just talking about birthing natural children, but about what can be birthed into regions. The region is always positioned to give birth and to multiply.

> ***Isaiah 49:2*** *And he hath made my mouth like a sharp sword; in the shadow of his hand hath he hid me, and made me a polished shaft; in his quiver hath he hid me;*

Sharp is *hadad* in the Hebrew and means "*to be fierce, to be alert, keen, piercing.*" Since our mouths are sharp swords, it is a literal cutting instrument, a knife, dagger, an axe, or shall we say a weapon. A fierce, keen, piercing weapon. If God has hid you in the shadow of his hand, then his hand is in front of you and you are like an illusion behind his hand. As he has you hid in his hand, he has made you like a polished shaft. A shaft is an arrow or staff. *Polished* means he has chosen you and prepared you for this work and to be a weapon in this region. What this means is, when we are operating in the region and spheres of influence that God has ordained for our lives, we have authority to tower in destiny and in the entrepreneurial vision he has given us. When we are not in our proper region and sphere of influence, we endure a lot of warfare and hardship. We are striving to birth in a region that does not know us, and where God has not deposited anything about us that can be produced in our midst.

Many do not have or understand this revelation and tend to want to live or produce destiny where they desire with no regard to what God is saying. Even Jesus had a heart to minister and be a blessing in his home town, but the people lacked unbelief.

> ***Matthew 13:53-58*** *And it came to pass, that when Jesus had finished these parables, he departed thence. And when he was come into his own country, he taught them in their synagogue, insomuch that they were astonished, and said, Whence hath this man this wisdom, and these mighty works? Is not this the carpenter's son? is not his mother called Mary? and his brethren, James, and Joses, and Simon, and Judas? And his sisters, are they not all with us? Whence then hath this man all these things? And they were offended in him. But Jesus said unto them, A prophet is not without honour, save in his own country, and in his own house. And he did not many mighty works there because of their unbelief.*

Despite being born in this country, the region did not know Jesus' name. Also, the words that were associated with Jesus as savior were not published in the womb of the region. Therefore, instead of believing and having faith, the people and the region wreaked with unbelief. This hindered Jesus from being able to effectively produce in the lives of the people and in the region. He was also dishonored and despised, despite being a prophet and astounding the people with his teachings and wisdom. Rather than embrace him, they debased him as a carpenter's son and was offended by him. They did not see him for the savior of the world that he was called to be.

- ❖ You may be born in a city but that may not be the place you are to journey in destiny or produce your entrepreneurial vision.
- ❖ You may desire to live in a particular city, state, or nation, but make sure God wants you to live there.
- ❖ You may want to do online ministry, but if your name and destiny has not been published in those spheres, it may produce minimal fruit, or if it does produce fruit, it may not be unto the glory of God.
- ❖ You may want to minister, teach, etc., in a particular city, state, or nation, but make sure God has published your name there so you can have authority and perform many miracles, signs, and wonders for his glory.

Whatever we produce without God's imprint, we can contend we are giving him glory, but he is not receiving glory from it. God does not accept strange fire – not even if it resembles his true workings or is done with good intentions.

> **1Chronicles 13:9-11** *And when they came unto the threshing floor of Chidon, Uzza put forth his hand to hold the ark; for the oxen stumbled. And the anger of the LORD was kindled against Uzza, and he smote him, because he put his hand to the ark: and there he died before God. And David was displeased, because the LORD had made a breach upon Uzza: wherefore that place is called Perezuzza to this day.*

Two violations were made in this passage of scripture as God had a specific vision and blueprint for how the ark should be carried, which did not include the ark being carried by an ox cart. This was a violation of the Old Testament requirement that the Ark was to be carried by staves and placed upon the shoulders of the men of Levi, of the family of Kohath (***Num. 3:30-31; 4:15; 7:9; Exod. 25:14-15***). Uzza touched the Ark. This violated ***Numbers 4:15***, which states that if the holy things are touched, the penalty is death, and that the carrying of the ark is to be a burden upon the sons of Kohath. These were the children of the Levi priest who were responsible for handling the sacred things of God.

> **Numbers 4:15** *And when Aaron and his sons have made an end of covering the sanctuary, and all the vessels of the sanctuary, as the camp is to set forward; after that, the sons of Kohath shall come to bear it: but they shall not touch any holy thing, lest they die. These things are the burden of the sons of Kohath in the tabernacle of the congregation.*

God has a specific blueprint and design for how we are to journey in destiny and produce his vision in the earth. Not implemented as he desires, can cause an altering of destiny and the vision and even death. Many people equate their success to the progress they are making and the fruit their destiny and vision is producing. God equates success by obedience and whether we are producing his designed will in the earth. If Uzza had not died, David and Israel would have thought implementing their new ideas without consulting God was okay. They would have thought handling God's glory however they deem fit was okay. We have to understand that our destiny and entrepreneurial vision is a representation of God's glory. We cannot handle it however we desire. We cannot implement whatever ideas and blueprints we want and think he will be pleased. We must consult him, even to the bare minimum of where the vision should be birthed. And we must trust that if that is God's purpose, he will bless us and fulfill us.

Deuteronomy 28:6 Blessed shalt thou be when thou comest in, and blessed shalt thou be when thou goest out.

Psalms 121:8 The LORD shall preserve thy going out and thy coming in from this time forth, and even for evermore.

In addition to the region, it is important to know what spheres of influence God has ordained for you. Spheres of influence may be groups of people, communities, cities, nations, spiritual realms, he has called you to influence and produce in that may not be the specific region you live in. It is important to understand that social media is a sphere of influence. They are also spiritual realms to which we can have influence or produce God's purpose in the earth. We must understand that the spiritual realms of social media are natural and even universal. Therefore, we must be cognizant of the principalities and powers we may combat because of the openness and expanded capacity of these realms. We must pray and seek God for revelation as to whether our name and vision is implanted in these realms, and how to govern and properly operate in destiny and produce our entrepreneurial vision. This is essential to making sure God gets glory as we draw those who are to partake of our destiny and entrepreneurial vision, and advance his kingdom in the earth.

Journal the revelation you received from this chapter.

_____
_____
_____
_____
_____
_____
_____
_____
_____
_____

Ask God what region and spheres of influences are connected to your destiny. Journal what he says.

Ask God what thoughts and proclamations he has placed in your region and spheres of influence. Journal what he says.

Explore with God any challenges you have with him regarding where he desires you to live and to produce your destiny and entrepreneurial vision in the earth. Ask him to fulfill you in the region he has called you to and how you can continuously make sure you are fulfilled in your region and spheres of influence. Ask him to give you peace about living and producing the vision where he desires.

___

Repent for any words you may have spoken against the regions and spheres of influence God has ordained for you. Journal the reasons you spoke these words. Journal three scriptures to counterattack these words. Decree them out loud into your region and spheres of influence.

___

Break the powers of any negative words that have been spoken about you from others in your region or spheres of influence.

Declare your declaration of independence into your region constantly and anything else God reveals to you concerning what he has published in your region and spheres of influence about you.

Command your region to work with you to produce your destiny and entrepreneurial vision. Command your region to bless you and to manifest the fruit, blessings, plans, and purposes of God concerning you, your entrepreneurial vision, and regarding your region as a whole.

DELIVERANCE FROM SELF-SABATOGE

One of the biggest enemies of destiny and walking in your entrepreneurial vision is not devils, and haters, but self-sabotage. Often it is our own inadequacies, fears, laziness, lack of follow through and perseverance, disobedience, character flaws, and unhealed wounds that abort or hinder the fullness of our destiny and entrepreneurial vision from coming forth. The biggest gift you can give your self is to get with God and let him heal you in your identity issues and soul wounds, and as he shows you yourself, practice loving through his identity and character standards for your life.

Dictionary.com defines *sabotage* as:
1. the act of destroying or damaging something deliberately so that it does not work correctly
2. any underhand interference with production, work, etc., in a plant, factory, etc., as by enemy agents during wartime or by employees during a trade dispute
3. any undermining of a cause

Some of the strongholds that operate under self-sabotage are:
- **Need To Control** -Want to control everything; they are their own god.
- **Perfectionism** – want everything a certain way or abort everything as if it was not good or beneficial.
- **Broken Identity** – Operate through wounded spirit, false loyalties or false perceptions; wounds dictate, weaken, hinder, and contaminate destiny and their vision.
- **Blame Projectors** – Operate through a wounded spirit; blames others for their mistakes or lack of progress; take no responsibility for the changes and potential to change, yet claim to desire destiny, govern a vision, or lead others.
- **Fear Mentality** – Fear of the unknown, doubt, unbelief, timid with stepping out on faith and being obedient in what God directs you to do, constant worry and suspicion, pessimism, expecting negative things to occur; unable to accept reassurance from people and from God, blocked by fear by the ability to be encouraged.
- **False Reality** - Live from the delusional or worldly loyalty/perception rather than from God's truth and reality.
- **The Resentful** - Difficult time forgiving or letting go of the past; cannot embrace success or the potential of the future.
- **Mental Instability** - Addicted to drama, confusion, chaos; cannot handle peace or when goodness is unfolding in their lives; can be stuck in past trauma, therefore, cannot progress forward in destiny and life's vision.
- **The Sluggard** – Lazy, make constant excuses for a lack of progress, slow to move and be obedient as there is a presumption that an easier plan or route will manifest, or that it will just happen without work; sleep during seasons where working and advancing the vision is essential.
- **Entitlement** – Think people, the world, and God owe you something, especially if you have had a challenging life or some challenging experiences. Overstep

boundaries by expecting people and life to hand you something rather than working for it.
- **Disobedient** – Do not do as God leads then justify disobedience. Thinks grace covers disobedience; implement own standards and twisting of the word to justify disobedience.
- **Rejecters** – Reject self, reject God, reject the vision, reject who God puts in their lives, while constantly sabotaging their destiny and entrepreneurial visions
- **Insecurity** – perceptions and behaviors of inadequacy, inaptness, unworthiness, low self-esteem, self-defeat, fear of speaking up, fear of failure, need for man's approval and validation, lack of temperance, plague destiny and the entrepreneurial vision.
- **Pride** – haughtiness, stubbornness, self-idolatry, glory stealing, lust for fame, lust for platform, lust for position, lust for power hinders destiny and the entrepreneurial vision.
- **Perversion** – adultery, fornication, inordinate affections, lusts, sexual appetites, worldly desires, addictions, sabotage destiny and the entrepreneurial vision.
- **Procrastinators** – talk a good game, but do not follow through with goals; are not accountable to themselves, destiny, the vision, God, or those that they are called to; time wasters, easily distracted, lazy, slothful, make excuses for laziness, delay destiny by delaying working consistently on goals.

I placed the need to control and perfectionism under self-sabotage because they hinder our ability to submit and rest in God as we journey in destiny and in our entrepreneurial vision. We can be our own sabotage, and can endure sabotage from people and demonic forces. The biggest way we become our own sabotage is by trying to control our own destiny and entrepreneurial vision. We get the plans from God, then we try to dictate how, when, where, what, and with whom it should unfold. We strive to control the process and progress. We become our own God, while trying to implement a destiny and vision that another God – not us - the ultimate God – created and ordained. Playing both roles can be stressful, exhausting, and will eventually cause us to burnout and even quit.

Perfectionism can definitely cause a person to sabotage their destiny and the entrepreneurial vision. When operating in perfectionism versus a spirit of excellence, a person:

- Is striving and working through their own strength rather than the strength of God and the mantle that is on their lives
- Imposes unrealistic demands on self and others that are impossible to obtain
- Create unrealistic standards on themselves because they have no concept of healthy development with time, practice, and study
- Focused on excelling rather than processing with God
- Serve their ambition rather than God's vision
- Place undue pressure upon themselves to perform and excel, which causes stress, burdens, and afflictions
- Mistake unnecessary burdens as the weight of their mantle; they then become

bewitched into believing that their will and standards are God's will and standards
- Yield to fear as the person thinks God is challenged with them when they do not live up to their self-imposed expectations. It is not God who is challenged, it is the person's own soul operating against their identity, while succumbing to condemnation, shame and guilt, and inferiority due to not meeting their own unrealistic expectations
- Is being formed in the image of their personal perception of what perfection is, rather than the image of God
- Focuses on running away from failure rather than resting in the place of excellence in God where success is inevitable
- Aims to attain a false reality of perfection rather than the truth of destiny, the vision and who God created us to be
- Risk destroying the God identity and destiny of others as they are focused on meeting their will and standards rather than God's standards

The bible does not tell us that we have to control our own fate or that we need to be perfect, as God is the one that can perfect those things which concerns us (***Psalms 138:8***). The bible does tell us to operate in a spirit of excellence.

> **<u>Daniel 5:12</u>** *Forasmuch as an excellent spirit, and knowledge, and understanding, interpreting of dreams, and shewing of hard sentences, and dissolving of doubts, were found in the same Daniel, whom the king named Belteshazzar: now let Daniel be called, and he will shew the interpretation.*

> **<u>Daniel 6:3</u>** *This Daniel was preferred above the presidents and princes, because an excellent spirit was in him; and the king thought to set him over the whole realm.*

<u>Excellent is *yatiyr* in the Hebrew and means:</u>
1. preeminent; as an adverb, very: — exceeding, excellent
2. pre-eminent (superior, distinguished, towering), surpassing, extreme
3. extraordinary, exceedingly, extremely

<u>Dictionary.com defines *excellent* as:</u>
1. possessing outstanding quality or superior merit; remarkably good
2. Archaic. extraordinary; superior

Leave the perfecting to God and allow him to bless your excellence.

People who operate in self-sabotage succumb to a lot of stopping and starting patterns as it relates to destiny and their entrepreneurial vision. They have a hard time committing to God, to destiny and to the vision. And it is not because of any outside forces. They are their enemy. Their need to control and fear of the unknown causes them to be in their own way. If you struggle with self-sabotage of any kind, it is important to receive deliverance and acquire strategies for how to walk in faith with God, before launching an entrepreneurial vision. Deliverance and inner healing is needed to cleanse and uproot the toxins of self-sabotage. It is not just a demonic spirit at work, but the characteristics are often intertwined in one's personality, and new behaviors and patterns have to be implemented to restructure the personality into the likeness of healthiness of God. Because self-sabotage operates like a covenant, a divorce and constant dejection and refusal to participate in the characteristics of sabotage is needed for true deliverance to be maintained. A person must be aware of what elements of self-sabotage is operating in his or her personality, they can counterattack them with God's truth regarding his or her destiny and calling. Moreover a person's thoughts, will, and action has to agree with God's plan for his or her life so that when faced with sabotage, they will give no room to this enemy. Today we decree no more self-sabotage. We get out of our own way and SHIFT fully into the destiny and vision of God for our lives.

What strongholds of self-sabotage do you tend to operate in? Be okay with searching yourself in this area. Ask God for the underlying roots to your challenges of self-sabotage. Journal what he says. Spend time renouncing, binding ,casting out, and cleansing yourself of the roots and fruits of these challenges. Fill yourself up with the God's truth and fruit that are counters to these issues. Consistently keep these issues before the Lord until you see breakthrough and until you are manifesting God's truth and fruit in your daily life. Seek a deliverance minister if you cannot break free on your own.

Journal any strategies, character improvements, etc., God gives you to practice so you can totally annihilate self-sabotage in your life. Inform your accountability partners, coverings and mentors of the changes you need to make in this area, so they can assist you in progressing and maintaining your deliverance.

CONQUERING DESTINY KILLING SPIRITS

John 10:10 *The thief cometh not, but for to steal, and to kill, and to destroy: I am come that they might have life, and that they might have it more abundantly.*

The destiny killing spirit attacks personally and generationally. It wants to kill your destiny, and any way God's plan for your life impacts your success, advancement, lineage, and present and future generations. This spirit usually begins its attack at a young age, even at birth, and then attempts to kill the person's identity, purpose, and hope at a young age. This is the reason so many Christians, especially leaders, experience challenging childhoods. The enemy is striving to kill the person before they realize there is a plan for their lives.

Most parents tend to cultivate a child's talents and giftings, rather than really seek God about the child's purpose and destiny. This allows the destiny killing spirit to have free reign in our lives and families. As we grow older, these spirits track us. We tend to encounter them at school, at college, on our jobs, in the community, and even in ministry. Sometimes, this spirit will get quiet and then as soon as we begin to pursue destiny consistently, commit to our entrepreneurial vision, demonstrate some progress and success, or there is a significant SHIFT occurring in our lives, it raises its ugly head in effort to put us back in our place of stagnation, hopelessness, and destruction. This is a familiar family spirit that has often been in the family line for years. It usually is striving to control you, intimidate you, block you, terrorize you, deplete you, castrate you, and totally destroy you such that there is no trace of what you have done and who you are. This spirit thinks it has a right to you, and that is because you have not taken control over it. You allow it to follow you, wreak havoc, and because you have not discerned its tactics, it just hangs out on your journey in life. I pray reading this makes you appalled and angry, because that is what you should be, APPALLED AND ENRAGED.

Everyone's destiny killing spirit is different. For some people it could be Jezebel, for others it could be Goliath. For another it could be Death and Hell. It often depends on what your purpose is in life and the spirits attached to you and your lineage. I have battled the spirit of death as a destiny killing spirit. This spirit would terrorize me in my dreams from a young age, strangle me in my sleep, afflict me with incurable diseases, kill my success and progress as I journey through life. I HATE THIS SPIRIT AND IT HATES ME! It has come in many ways in my life and for the most part I have annihilated its powers. It knows that it cannot kill me, so now it strives to weary me, distract me, and afflict me. That is how this spirit operates, if it cannot kill you, it will strive to weary you, deplete you, instill fear in you, discourage you, render you hopeless and helpless, where you have no power to fight or assert authority over it. It will also seek to inflict shame and guilt by making you think you are powerless against it constantly wreaking havoc on your life. Know that you have power over this devil and all devils (*Luke 10:19*). YOU HAVE POWER AND WILL NULLIFY EVERY DESTINY KILLING SPIRIT! SHIFT!

Strategy for annihilating the destiny killing spirit:

- First you have to identify the destiny killing spirit/s. These spirits usually follow you throughout your life.
- You have to understand that your fight is not with situations and people who are being used by the destiny killing spirits, but in the spirit realm. You must deal with destiny killing spirits in warfare and intercession. Otherwise, you are basically tackling symptoms by dealing with people, but the spirit just keeps tracking you throughout life and causing the same or similar situations to occur in other areas of your life.
- You have to close any generational and personal doors that give way to the destiny killing spirit. Search God for how it got a foothold in your family line. Search God for the reason it wants to destroy your destiny. Break its power and authority over your generational line and over your life. For a time, consistently declare out that it has no power and authority over you and your generational line and command all powers, rights, covenants, vows, curses regarding the destiny killing spirit to be destroyed. Even dismantle patterns and how it may have tracked other family members and wreaked havoc in their lives.
- Cancel all their assignments, plots and plans against you, your destiny, and lineage. Close doors and entry ways to how they use life situations and people to attack you. Declare eternal amnesia to destiny killing spirits, watchers, squatters, principalities, territorial spirits and powers, such that all information collected against you is wiped from the memory of demons, wicked people, and people being used by demonic agents. Loose the fire of God to destroy all computer systems, data banks, libraries, file cabinets, covens, etc., that have information stored about you.
- Spend time consistently decreeing out loud your authority over these spirits and any spirit that would attack your destiny. Strengthen your authority by acquiring warfare scriptures to stand on regarding your authority over demonic forces.
- Ask your accountability tribe to war and intercede with you against these destiny killing spirits. Especially in instances where you are weary and need fortification with warring and contending for victory.
- Discern work, ministerial and business patterns to which these spirits attack. Learn the necessary keys, tools, and skills, where you can conquer in these areas such that they give no room to these demons. You may need to improve your communication skills, conflict resolution skills, build your confidence where you stand during times of confrontation. You may need to choose better friends, better work or ministry environments, etc., improve some things about your character, or you just need to be bold in the authority of the Lord and beat this demon down. God can show you where you need to mature if necessary.

- ❖ Ask God for a strategy on how to keep this spirit from rearing its ugly head in your future. If it does show up, do not fret, use this strategy and any strategy the Lord gives to put this demon back under your feet where it belongs.
- ❖ Knowing your authority over these spirits is your greatest weapon against them. Stand in your authority and refuse to live under subjection to their workings in your life.

What are the destiny killings spirits that attack you? What reasons do these specific spirits attack you?

_____
_____
_____
_____
_____
_____
_____
_____
_____
_____
_____
_____
_____
_____
_____

List the patterns to which they have manifested throughout your life from childhood until now.

_____
_____
_____
_____
_____
_____
_____
_____
_____
_____

List patterns of how they have attacked your family members.

_____
_____
_____
_____
_____
_____
_____
_____
_____
_____
_____
_____
_____
_____
_____
_____

Use the strategy above to begin contending for victory. Journal your experiences. Journal the victories and progress and any ways you need to further contend to annihilate these spirits. It may take some time to totally defeat them. These spirits have tracked you for years. It will take time to close the doors and break the patterns and connections they have made with other spirits to keep tabs on you. It may also take time to dismantle every way they have intertwined in your life.

_____
_____
_____
_____
_____
_____
_____
_____
_____
_____
_____
_____

Journal what God shares with you regarding how to open doors, how to close doors, break covenants, vows, curses, etc.

___

Journal the strategies God gives you to further annihilate these destiny killing spirits.

___

Journal the areas you need to change about your character, interactions, social settings, relationships, and acquaintances to further weed these spirits out your life.

___

WARFARE STRATEGIES

It is important to understand that when you commit to destiny and to producing your entrepreneurial vision in the earth, you will be faced with even greater demonic opposition than what you already experienced as a child of God. This is to be expected as *Matthew 11:12* contends: *And from the days of John the Baptist until now, the Kingdom of Heaven suffereth violence, and the violent take it by force.* We must take destiny by force, and we must implement God's purpose and plans into the earth by force. That word *force* means to *seize*. Our destiny and entrepreneurial vision is not a negotiation. It is not a compromise. We are not striving to share destiny with devils. Please know the enemy is not trying to negotiate, compromise, or share space. He is roaming about seeking whom he may devour (*1Peter 5:8*). We have legal authority to possess dominion in the earth by whatever spiritual force necessary.

> *Ephesians 6:12-13 For we wrestle not against flesh and blood, but against principalities, against powers, against the rulers of the darkness of this world, against spiritual wickedness in high places.*

Much of your destiny contending is in the spiritual realms with real demons who do not want to give up their ranks and only want to lay hold of what is rightfully yours. You can act like devils do not exists, they do not fight against you, you can just praise your way through, but none of this prevents the enemy from attacking you. It just makes it easier to attack you and makes it easier for him to lay claim of everything you refuse to seize. You should embrace warfare as part of your destiny lifestyle. But even as you embrace it, you do not have to tolerate it. Though some reject warfare, many folks like to brag about the warfare they endure. They deem it as a badge of honor of how anointed they are. While they are boasting about their anointing, the enemy is beating them up and wreaking havoc in their lives. We should always be seeking God for how to tower over the enemy. There is always a strategy for dismantling the works of darkness. The more we assert authority over the enemy, the easier it is to tower in destiny.

> *2Corinthians 10:4-5 For the weapons of our warfare are not carnal, but mighty through God to the pulling down of strong holds; Casting down imaginations, and every high thing that exalteth itself against the knowledge of God, and bringing into captivity every thought to the obedience of Christ.*

As we assert our authority over darkness that beset us, we bring it into obedience where it is subject to God's word and purpose in our lives. What used to control us is now under our control. We bring low everything that thinks it is above God's will and purpose for our lives. I could give you countless warfare strategies to help you tower in destiny. But it will be important to seek God for yourself, so he can give you correct weaponry for each season and situation in your life. Your weapons will change and may not even be what you would consider a weapon or effective strategy. But God's ways are not like ours and they are not like the devils. His weapons are not carnal as even his weapon of love, joy, praise, etc. can annihilate the enemy.

> *1John 4:18 There is no fear in love; but perfect love casteth out fear: because fear hath torment. He that feareth is not made perfect in love.*

> *Isaiah 61:3 To appoint unto them that mourn in Zion, to give unto them beauty for ashes, the oil of joy for mourning, the garment of praise for the spirit of heaviness; that they might be called trees of righteousness, the planting of the Lord, that he might be glorified.*

The Lord's very presence – his glory – can be a weapon against the enemy.

> *Psalms 84:11 For the LORD God is a sun and shield: the LORD will give grace and glory: no good thing will he withhold from them that walk uprightly.*

> *Psalms 91:1-2 Whoever dwells in the shelter of the Most High will rest in the shadow of the Almighty. I will say of the Lord, "He is my refuge and my fortress, my God, in whom I trust.*

The Lord may have you enter into warfare with the enemy as a stealth bomber. A stealth bomber goes in subtle and undetected then -blasts the enemy, so you will be subtle and unassuming. As the Holy Spirit leads, you SHIFT and begin to blast the enemy with warfare strategy.

> *Psalms 18:28-29 For thou wilt light my candle: the Lord my God will enlighten my darkness. For by thee I have run through a troop; and by my God have I leaped over a wall.*

I did not share those to give you warfare strategies, but so you could understand the fullness of God's word when he says his weapons are not carnal. His word is full of strategies and weapons to defeat the enemy, and he can reveal what weapons, keys, and strategies you need to deal with the warfare of your destiny and life's vision. Depending on what your calling is and the vision you are releasing in the earth, you can experience warfare from:

- ❖ *High Ranking Demons* (Principalities, territorial spirits, and powers from your region and spheres of influence)
- ❖ *Familiar Spirits & Bondages* (Generational strongholds within your family line)
- ❖ *Destiny Killing Spirits* (Generational or personal curses and spirits assigned to thwart your destiny)
- ❖ *Spirits Of The Thief* (Thieving, depleting, illegal spirits and people that come to steal your seeds, fruit, harvest, momentum, progress, vision *Proverbs 6:31*)
- ❖ *Vampire Spirits* (Spirits that come to drain your energy, giftings, and suck the life out of you so you cannot work & sustain in the vision)
- ❖ *Python Spirits* (Spirits that come to slowly squeeze the life out of you and the vision. This spirit comes as depression, heaviness, financial hardship, subtle drainage of an area/s of your life and vision- google and study this spirit so you can combat it)
- ❖ *Serpent Spirits* (Do not commune with snakes. They slither up to you and offer you fame, power, money, and enlightenment that is ahead of the timing of God or not

the will of God. God has foundational laws and boundaries. Though he changes, the foundation of who he is never changes. Be careful of people and opportunities that strive to get you to go against something God commanded you not to do or that is against God's character and nature; see *Genesis 2:16-17, Genesis 3:4-8*)

- *Mammon, Poverty, & Spirits of Lack* (Attacks your mindset & perceptions about money as it relates to life and the vision, and attacks your finances, resources, and connections; can cause frivolous spending, poor financial decision making, focus on money rather than the vision, fear of sowing and being a cheerful giver)
- *Leviathan Spirit* (This is a haughty, strong, stubborn, prideful spirit. It works through a boastful arrogance of superiority and draws people into negativity by attacking communication, dialogue, and frequencies between people and systems, cause confusion as you are speaking, and you are striving to communicate with people or your audience; can work with zapping spirit, spirit of darkness, stuttering spirit to cause forgetfulness, slurred and staggered speech intended to cause unnecessary stress, frustration and drama. This spirit tends to find an open door of those dealing with pride or false pride that is underlying insecurity. Once it finds its prey or airway, it wreaks havoc. It also works with the whispering spirit to cause murmuring, discontentment, mocking, and confusion. Leviathan can attack as a principality depending on the region or sphere of influence it is over. It is also known to attack at night, by sending haughty taunts, threats, bewitchment, triand gestures to get people to prove themselves, while yielding to prideful and self-glory behavior. *Psalm 104:25-26, Ezekiel 29:3-5, Psalm 74:13-14, Isaiah 27:1*).
- *Spirit Of The Hydra* (This is a serpent spirit with many heads to which you cut the head off and it just grows back with extra heads. Cannot just cut the head off this spirit, but cut the tail off, as cutting this, cuts off its ability to restore itself. This spirit comes to weary and wear you out and have you dealing with the same issue over and over again with an increased intensity each time you strive to resolve the matter by dealing with the head or symptoms, rather than the root of the matter. Deal with the foundation and the root, cut off it is seed supply and you kill its regeneration process).
- *Spirit Of The Crab* (This spirit moves sideways and never forward. It attempts to get you to do this as well. It uses its claws to pull you down or off the correct path with God every time you gain some progress and momentum in God. It pulls you to a place of sidetracking, backsliding, regression, or to stifle your success and advancement where you are working on the same thing over and over again, while never progressing or moving past a certain point in your life. Break this spirit's legs, as it uses its claws of words, belittlement, error, obligation, plan B, sin, poverty and low level mindsets and behaviors, etc., to snatch you back down to its downgraded level or a level beneath God's will for your life).
- *Spirits of Control & Jezebel* (Spirits that come to control, manipulate, alter, and even steal the word and plan of God for the vision)
- *Spirits Of Sabotage* (Self sabotage, sabotage from the enemy & people)
- *Spirit Of The Waster* (Spirits that cause you to waste finances, resources, time, gifts, energy, on things that are not a part of the vision or come to steal your focus in consistently working the vision)

- *Spirit of Radon* (Attacks communications systems such as microphones, speakers, music and technical equipment, phones, computers, where they do not function properly and even break; can work with leviathan and spirits of confusion)
- *Time Stealing Spirits* (Procrastination, Stagnation, Sluggardness, Laziness)
- *Blocking Spirits* (Spirits that hinder you from getting started, progressing, having destiny moments, finishing assignments and/or fully bringing a vision to pass)
- *Spirit Of Assumptions* (Spirits and mindsets that keep you bound in assumptions about people, situations, etc., rather than seeking God specifically for his will regarding the vision.
- *Spirits of Distraction* (Spirits, mindsets, and situations that come to steal your focus and zeal)
- *Spirits of Harassment* (Hounds of hell that come at specific times to harass and cower you into thwarting the vision)
- *Witchcraft* (Witches and warlocks who pray and cast spells against God's kingdom and his people)
- *Bewitching Spirits* (Spirits that steal or bind your mind, so you cannot receive revelation, guidance, or strategies for bringing the vision to past; these spirits also cast spells, so you become double minded, mentally challenged, and hopeless, regarding the vision and about the things of the Lord)
- *Time Release Curses* (Generational or personal curses sent or established at specific times of the year and seasons to thwart your destiny)
- *Friendly Fire* (Challenges, contention, conflict, drama, betrayal, neglect, from those who should support you, once supported you, or those within the body of Christ)
- *Psychological Warfare* (Psychological and mental strongholds and demons who have set themselves as vain imaginations against the word of God for your life and destiny)
- *Religion & Tradition* (Religious and traditional spirits and systems who want to oppose your unique destiny and vision)
- *Babylon* (The world's system and worldly people who do not want God's kingdom established in the earth)
- *For The Gospel Sake* (Persecution that comes from preaching and proclaiming the gospel of Jesus Christ)
- *Spirit Of The Hater* (Jealous people, stupid people, ignorant people who are open doors for demons to use against you)
- *Fleshly Laws Causing Wars Within Your Members* (Your flesh, unhealed wounds, and inner man that has to be sacrificed and subjected to your spirit in order to submit to your destiny and entrepreneurial vision process *Romans 7:23*)
- *Prides Of Life* (Through your circumstances sent to confound and stress your life and relationships)

Sometimes warfare battles can manifest as the following:

- Where you are sieged and closed in on every side
- A psychological and mental battle that comes to steal your truth, your emotional balance and your mind

- Oppression where it is laying on top of you, burdensome, restrained, weighty, troubled, subdued, suppressed, crushed, pressed against
- Possession where something has entered your soul, heart, mind, body, home, life, ministry, circumstance
- Infestation where you feel contaminated, impure, slimed by the roots, fruits, and injections of demons, darkness, witchcraft, worldliness, perversion, evil
- Depression where you experience gloom, sullenness, dejection, demoted, low in spirit, dispirited, low in value, weak, loss of energy, loss of stamina, dull, hopelessness, helplessness, suicidal; feel pressed down
- Blocked where a literal wall or demonic force is erected in your path; this barrier can be physical or spiritual. Sometimes it makes the spirit realm look black or dark because you are looking at a wall. It can also make God and heaven seem far away due to the barrier erected between you and God. May feel blocked in going forward in destiny or the entrepreneurial vision
- Blinded or bound in the mind. This often feels like something is spiritually wrapped around your head or over your eyes where you cannot see. It can feel like a vice grip on the head or a demonic head piece. Sometimes it can be an octopus spirit, squid spirit, or python spirit. Sometimes it can be a demonic device. It can also feel like it is wrapped around the brain
- Suffocated where you feel like a demonic yoke is binding you, choking you, suffocating you, and strangling you
- Anxious where you feel consistently worried, anxious, restless, unable to sleep, rest, believe God
- Fearful and panicked where you feel nervous, scared, terrorized, like something is following you or after you, fear going to sleep, experience night terrors, night attacks, and nightmares in your sleep; may experience literal panic attacks
- Distraction that comes to steal your focus, strength, drain you of your stamina and progress. Draining spirits also attack, especially through people who suck the life out of you, deplete you, steal your strength and virtue
- Caged, snared, incantated, boxed in. Witchcraft spells, hexes, and vexes often have this affect. Also, when the enemy attempts to imprison us or our goods, we can feel this way
- Perversion such that you have floods of sexual and vile thoughts and images that are not your own. You did not watch anything, or engage in anything. Sometimes we experience this when we are picking up strongholds in the atmosphere. Sometimes the enemy sends these attacks to shame us or to get us to open a door to lust, perversion, adultery, fornication, masturbation, inordinacy, etc.
- Demonic visitations, demonic dreams, dream manipulators, agents, & importers who attack while you are sleeping
- Spirit realm attacks during sleep or when being translated in the spirit to engage in warfare, intercession or kingdom work

It does not matter how the enemy comes, know God can give you strategies and weapons to defeat him. Ask God to teach you how to be a skilled warrior (***Psalms 18:34, Psalms 144:1***). Also, be mindful to be full of God's word and Holy Spirit as these weapons alone can enable you to stand against the enemy.

List ways you have experienced spiritual warfare?

What strategies has God given you to defeat your adversary?

Assess the current warfare you may be experiencing. Ask God to give you unique strategies to defeat the enemy.

SPIRITUAL CLEANSING!
MAINTAINING DELIVERANCE!

As you progress in destiny and with releasing your entrepreneurial vision, it will be important to take time to deliver, heal, and cleanse yourself and the vision of anything that has infected your destiny and vision. Negative attributes and strongholds will have to be consistently gutted out of the foundation, the womb, the heart, mind, soul, body, the physical atmosphere and climate of you and your vision. You also may need to cleanse some spiritual areas of your region and your spheres of influence to further advance the vision. This is important because even though this book teaches you how to progress successfully in your destiny and calling, there are some seasons where you may have tares growing with your fruit and harvest (Study *Matthew 13:24-30*). You will need to know how to cleanse out the tares without destroying your fruit and harvest. This chapter provides tools and strategies for how to do just that. It will discuss the importance of spiritual cleansing, while providing you with keys to breakthrough.

> *Matthew 10:8 Heal the sick, cleanse the lepers, raise the dead, cast out devils: freely ye have received, freely give.*

<u>Leprosy</u> in the Greek is *leora* and means:
1. scaliness, leprosy
2. the most offensive, annoying, dangerous, cutaneous disease
3. the virus of which generally pervades the whole body, common in Egypt and the East

<u>Cleanse</u> is *katharizo* in the Greek and means:
1. make clean, cleanse
   a) from physical stains and dirt
      - utensils, food
      - a leper, to cleanse by curing
      - to remove by cleansing
   b) in a moral sense
      - to free from defilement of sin and from faults
      - to purify from wickedness
      - to free from guilt of sin, to purify
      - to consecrate by cleansing or purifying
      - to consecrate, dedicate
2. to pronounce clean in a Levitical sense

Leprosy is an infectious disease that causes disfiguring sores, nerve damage, and progressive debilitation. In the bible, lepers, or those infected with leprosy, were outcasts because of fear and necessity. Leprosy has the potential to spread from person to person. If lepers were not isolated, then they were a threat to society due to contaminating others with leprosy.

Lepers are also isolated due to how others react to them. The manner in which the disease physically alters a person, the fear others had regarding how lepers looked, and fear of contracting what they had were factors in them being in isolation.

> ***Leviticus 13:45-46*** *And the leper in whom the plague is, his clothes shall be rent, and his head bare, and he shall put a covering upon his upper lip, and shall cry, Unclean, unclean. All the days wherein the plague shall be in him he shall be defiled; he is unclean: he shall dwell alone; without the camp shall his habitation be.*

> ***Numbers 5:1-3*** *And the LORD spake unto Moses, saying, Command the children of Israel, that they put out of the camp every leper, and everyone that hath an issue, and whosoever is defiled by the dead: Both male and female shall ye put out, without the camp shall ye put them; that they defile not their camps, in the midst whereof I dwell.*

Though the bible does not exactly speak this truth, the revelation is clear that the people viewed leprosy as God's wrath and judgment on a person's life due to sin. God may not have caused people to have leprosy, yet, the manner to which leprosy would affect our lives is the same way sin affects our lives. Lets' take some time to explore the comparison:

- Sin causes us to be unclean, impure, unhealthy.
- Our sin contaminates and influences others; it pollutes society and the world at large.
- We think people cannot see our sins, but sins can be seen in our presentation, disposition, personality, clothing, conversation, perceptions, communication, interactions, relationships, how we handle situations, and how we live our lives (Out of our heart flows the issues of life ***Proverbs 4:23***).
- Sin outcasts us from God's presence and his plan for our lives.
- Sin defames God and tarnishes his reputation, especially when we are living a life of sin, but contend we serve God.

When we consider the concept of cleansing the lepers or shall we say, cleansing sins, it is important to cleanse the infection and cleanse what is causing the infection.

> ***Matthew 8:1-4*** *When he was come down from the mountain, great multitudes followed him. And, behold, there came a leper and worshipped him, saying, Lord, if thou wilt, thou canst make me clean. And Jesus put forth his hand, and touched him, saying, I will; be thou clean. And immediately his leprosy was cleansed. And Jesus saith unto him, See thou tell no man; but go thy way, shew thyself to the priest, and offer the gift that Moses commanded, for a testimony unto them.*

A lot of times, we want to use will power to stop sinning or to cease from hurting. When using will power, we are operating through a well of self-control. You are striving to control your impulses and choices. But if you could not keep yourself from engaging in the sin, how can you stop yourself from never doing it again? We need Holy Ghost power!

> ***Ephesians 3:16*** *He would grant you, according to the riches of His glory, to be strengthened with power through His Spirit in the inner man.*

God's Holy Ghost power empowers us to grow strong, so we can withstand against sins and worldliness.

> ***The Amplified Bible*** *May He grant you out of the rich treasury of His glory to be strengthened and reinforced with mighty power in the inner man by the [Holy] Spirit [Himself indwelling your innermost being and personality].*

Even if you use your own will to stop sinning or to survive a wound, you are still unclean or broken if you do not allow God's Holy Ghost power to cleanse you from sin or to heal that wound.

In *Matthew 8:1-4*, Jesus laid hands on the lepers and they were made clean. This is miraculously awesome and is a form of deliverance and healing that many of us have experienced when encountering Jesus. Even with this miraculous cleansing, the leper still had to make a lifestyle change to remain clean.

- He could not return to the leper camp as he would risk being contaminated again.
- If his leprosy was a sin issue, then he had to reframe from that sin to maintain his deliverance and healing.
- Even as the leper's community had changed, his relationships and interactions had to be changed.

The leper's identity and lifestyle had to change to maintain his healing. Such a change requires a processing to wholeness. This requires a relationship with God beyond just the initial encounter of deliverance and healing. We have to journey with him in a lifestyle change, learn his plan for us in maintaining healing, and walk that plan out in our daily lifestyle.

This brings us to this scripture:

> ***Isaiah 64:6*** *But we are all as an unclean thing, and all our righteousnesses are as filthy rags; and we all do fade as a leaf; and our iniquities, like the wind, have taken us away.*

<u>Unclean is *tame* in the Hebrew and means:</u>
1. to be unclean, become unclean, become impure, regard as unclean
2. to be or become unclean, to defile oneself, be defiled
    - sexually
    - religiously
    - ceremonially
    - by idolatry
3. to profane (God's name)

<u>*Filth* is *ed* in the Hebrew and means:</u>
1. to set a period, the menstrual flux, soiling, filthy
2. menstruation
   - a filthy rag, stained garment
   - figuratively of best deeds of guilty people

The Amplified Bible *For we have all become like one who is unclean [ceremonially, like a leper], and all our righteousness (our best deeds of rightness and justice) is like filthy rags or a polluted garment; we all fade like a leaf, and our iniquities, like the wind, take us away [far from God's favor, hurrying us toward destruction].*

Even our righteousness needs cleaning in God's eyes. Just like we cleanse our physical body, we must cleanse our hearts, minds, thoughts, emotions, loins, foundation, and the inner man of things lodged in our flesh. When we cleanse our physical bodies, we are detailed in making sure we clean every part of our bodies. We even purchase the correct hygienic products to assist us with cleaning our bodies, while making sure we remain clean. And if a product does not work, we do not keep using it. We will try different products until we find out what products work best in keeping our bodies clean, vibrant, and fresh.

We need this same standard for our spiritual lives. And because our righteousness is filthy, we should be cleaning our soul, hearts, minds, and our inner man daily just like we do our physical bodies. For even when we think we are clean, to God we have things that we need to be cleansed from.

Lets' explore the Holy Spirit equipping you with healing techniques you can use to bring cleansing to your life and entrepreneurial vision.

- ***Infilling of the Holy Spirit*** **(Acts 1-2, Acts 13:22** *And the disciples were continually filled with joy and with the Holy Spirit*). All of us receive the Holy Spirit upon us when we accept Jesus as our personal savior. When I speak of infilling, I am referencing speaking in tongues where God's voice and power speaks through you and empowers you. When God's power flows through you, his voice equips you with greater heavenly sound and power to annihilate the enemy. There are somethings the enemy will not respond to in your voice, but he will if you speak in tongues. If you do not speak in tongues, begin to study the purpose of doing so, while asking the Holy Spirit to manifest his voice through you. If you do speak in tongues, practice praying in your prayer language for at least 30 to 60 minutes a day. I encourage people to speak in tongues the entire time they are in the shower or while they are driving to work. This is the perfect time because you are generally alone, and can focus on allowing the Holy Spirit to empower you. You do not have to know what you are saying or even have a prayer focus. The more you speak in tongues, the more you will know what you are saying, and the more the Holy Spirit will guide you in knowing what to pray for, against, and how to use your prayer language to cleanse yourself of the filth of the enemy.

- *Spirit of Lord* – Empowers you with the wisdom, revelation, knowledge, counsel, understanding, and guidance needed to handle your daily affairs and journey in a destiny lifestyle with the Lord. (*Isaiah 11:2 And the spirit of the LORD shall rest upon him, the spirit of wisdom and understanding, the spirit of counsel and might, the spirit of knowledge and of the fear of the LORD*). Declare continually that you are consumed in the spirit of wisdom, revelation, understanding, etc. Refuse to accept and cleanse all confusion, ignorance, foolery, witchcraft, bewitchment, mind control, mind blinding/binding, lack of knowing, lack of guidance, etc. Assert your right to have the spirit of the Lord teach you all things (*John 14:26 But the Comforter, which is the Holy Ghost, whom the Father will send in my name, he shall teach you all things, and bring all things to your remembrance, whatsoever I have said unto you*).

- *Blood of Jesus* – Purges, purifies, redeems, reconciles, sanctifies, sanitizes, forgives, heals, and frees you from death (*Ephesians 1:7 whom we have redemption through his blood, the forgiveness of sins, according to the riches of his grace*). We hear a lot about pleading the blood, but the blood is an application. Jesus applied his blood to our sins and sicknesses, and through his perfected blood, we were redeemed and made whole. You can apply the blood of Jesus to your soul, heart, mind, thoughts, personality, character, identity, righteousness, body, and command redemption, life, and wholeness to come. You can soak yourself in the blood until you see breakthrough in these areas, or as a daily application of being cleansed and free in God.

- *Binding, Loosing & Casting Out Devils* – Delivers you from demons, and strongholds (*Matthew 16:19 And I will give unto thee the keys of the kingdom of heaven: and whatsoever thou shalt bind on earth shall be bound in heaven: and whatsoever thou shalt loose on earth shall be loosed in heaven*). Bind means "to knit, chain, tie, and to fasten, put under subjection, to forbid, prohibit, declare to be illicit." Loose means to "loosen, cast off, break (up), destroy, dissolve, (un-)loose, melt, put off, to declare unlawful, to overthrow." You possess the power to bind up demons and demonic kingdoms, forbid them to remain in you and others. You can bind yourself, others, your ministry, your atmosphere, land and region to God and his kingdom. You can also loose yourself from demonic powers, and forbid and overthrow their workings in your life, lives of others, your ministry, your atmosphere, land, and region.

- *Casting Out Devils* – Deliverance ministry is a part of our right and health as believers of Jesus Christ. It is our daily manna and authority to be free of demons and their demonic stronghold. Jesus has given us power over all the power of the enemy. Cast out means to "*eject with violence, drive (out), expel, leave, pluck (pull, take, thrust) out, put forth (out), send away.*" We can cast the devil out of our lives and be free of his demonic fruit, filth, oppression, depression and possession.

    - *Matthew 10:8 Heal the sick, cleanse the lepers, raise the dead, cast out devils: freely ye have received, freely give.*
    - *Luke 10:19 Behold, I give unto you power to tread on serpents and scorpions, and over all the power of the enemy: and nothing shall by any means hurt you.*

- *Luke 11:20* *But if I with the finger of God cast out devils, no doubt the kingdom of God is come upon you.*

It is important to assert power and authority over the enemy because he is always trying to claim rights to us and what belongs to us. The devil is not passive and is always seeking to possess, devour, and destroy what is ours. We must be offensive and aggressive in letting him know that he cannot have our lives, families, ministries, atmosphere, land, regions, and nations.

- *Fruit of God* – Fills, restores, produces, reproduces (*Galatians 5:22-23 But the fruit of the Spirit is love, joy, peace, long suffering, gentleness, goodness, faith, Meekness, temperance: against such there is no law*). Cleanse yourself of all defiled, demonic, and unhealthy fruit that does not represent the character and nature of God, while filling yourself up in all the fruit that represents his character and nature.

- *Breaking Curses* – Provides personal, generational, regional, cultural freedom from negative words spoken over you, sent to you, or curses implemented due to personal and generational sins (*Galatians 3:13 Christ hath redeemed us from the curse of the law, being made a curse for us: for it is written, cursed is everyone that hangeth on a tree*).

  - Repent for personal, generational, regional, and cultural strongholds.
  - Loose the blood of Jesus to cleanse the curse and all filth associated with it.
  - Bind and cast out any spirits operating with the curse.
  - Declare your freedom through Jesus Christ (*2Corinthians 3:17 Now the Lord is that Spirit: and where the Spirit of the Lord is, there is liberty*).
  - Fill yourself back up with the fruit of God.

- *Word of God* – Discerns, divides what is of God and what is not of God, cuts out, does surgery, instills God's truth, will, and plan (*Hebrews 4:12 For the word of God is quick, and powerful, and sharper than any two-edged sword, piercing even to the dividing asunder of soul and spirit, and of the joints and marrow, and is a discerner of the thoughts and intents of the heart*).

  - Use the word of God to divide what is of God in your life from what is not of him.
  - Use the word of God to extract what is not of God from your soul, heart, mind, body, and spirit.
  - Use the word of God to overthrow every lie that the enemy uses to keep you bound to demons.
  - Use the word of God to cut out any word, character trait, hurt, pain, and flaw that keeps you bound to demons.
  - Spend time studying, meditating on, and soaking yourself in the word of God. Allow God's word to go inside of you (heart, mind, soul, identity), and cleanse everything that is contrary to the word of God for your life. Study and meditate on God's word and be refilled in his truth concerning your identity, purpose, destiny, and who he is as your daddy God.

- *Fire of God* – Burns out, fuses, refines, purges, purifies, consumes, and test (*Malachi 3:2-3 But who may abide the day of his coming? and who shall stand when he appeareth? for he is like a refiner's fire, and like fullers' soap: And he shall sit as a refiner and purifier of silver: and he shall purify the sons of Levi, and purge them as gold and silver, that they may offer unto the Lord an offering in righteousness*). Sometimes you will cast out demons, but their deposits and attributes are still lodged in you. Use the fire of God to purge and burn out these demonic deposits. You can also purify and refine yourself with the fire of God. Demons hate the fire of God and the blood of Jesus. Fire is judgment to demons. You can use the fire of God to torment demons and send them fleeing from your life, blood line, ministry, land, atmosphere, and region. (*Revelations 20:10 And the devil that deceived them was cast into the lake of fire and brimstone, where the beast and the false prophet are, and shall be tormented day and night for ever and ever*).

- *Fullers' Soap* – Is a washing by trampling, treading, stamping, scrubbing. It is likened to trampling or scrubbing something hard until it is clean. (*Malachi 3:2-3 But who may abide the day of his coming? and who shall stand when he appeareth? for he is like a refiner's fire, and like fullers' soap: And he shall sit as a refiner and purifier of silver: and he shall purify the sons of Levi, and purge them as gold and silver, that they may offer unto the Lord an offering in righteousness*). When there are things in you that require deep cleansing, use the fullers' soap of God to scrub and trample them out.

- *Power of God* – Delivers, overthrows demonic powers and governments, releases the virtue and government of God, releases miracles, signs, and wonders (*Acts 1:8 But ye shall receive power, after that the Holy Ghost comes upon you: and ye shall be witnesses unto me both in Jerusalem, and in all Judaea, and in Samaria, and unto the uttermost part of the earth*). Use the power of God to annihilate the powers of the enemy (*Luke 10:19 Behold, I give unto you power to tread on serpents and scorpions, and over all the power of the enemy: and nothing shall by any means hurt you*). Study the power of God as you will find that you have the ability to recreate and create body parts, birth forth things that you need, bring excellency to your heart, mind and soul, release virtue into your life, and annihilate the power of the enemy such that it brings deliverance and healing.

- *Glory of God* – Whatever we need and desire from God is inside his glory. The Glory refreshes, fills, refills, fulfills, creates, recreates, revives, renews, makes whole, establishes the presence of God, draws us into intimacy and relationship with God, while instilling God's character, nature, truth, knowledge, revelation, and pleasures forevermore (*Psalms 16:11 Thou wilt shew me the path of life: in thy presence is fulness of joy; at thy right hand there are pleasures for evermore*). You should be living inside the presence of God. This is where your direction of life is revealed. As you walk in alignment with God, continual fulness of joy and pleasures of God should be evident in your life. If you live in the glory of God, you should be living a fulfilled life no matter what trials and tribulations may occur. Ask God for revelation on how to build a relationship with him where you abide in his presence. Use his presence to refresh, fulfill, and fill you. Continually cultivate your life and atmosphere in his presence so you can be a true glory carrier (*John 15:4 Abide in me, and I in you. As the branch cannot bear fruit of itself, except it abide in the vine; no more can ye, except ye abide in me*).

- *Rivers of Living Water* – Stirs, replenishes, breeds life, vitality, beauty, youthfulness, creativity, strength, efficiency, and releases what is inside of you to whatever you are sending it to (*John. 7:38 He that believeth on me, as the scripture hath said, out of his belly shall flow rivers of living water*). It is important to spend time cleansing and stirring the rivers that are inside of you, such that the wells you flow out of are pure as whatever is in you will be released to those you minister too.

- *Pluck Out* – Roots out, pulls down, destroys, and throws down (*Jeremiah 1:10 See, I have this day set thee over the nations and over the kingdoms, to root out, and to pull down, and to destroy, and to throw down, to build, and to plant*). Some spirits and demonic attributes are imbedded in your foundation and need to be uprooted.

    o You can pluck out demons.
    o You can command demons and strongholds that are lodged deep within you to come up out of you by the root. Roots can even be generational so keep that in mind, or it can be a root in you that has been there for years.
    o You may have to cut the root in pieces then pull them out. You may have to pull down something such as pulling down strongholds, imaginations, and prideful spirits that have exalted themselves above God and may have even exalted themselves as idols in your life.

    You cannot be nice to demons and with wickedness. Your mission has to be to destroy them just like they want to destroy you. The devil understands he is in a fight and will throw you around like you are a piece of paper. You must enter your fight with him and be willing to toss him and trample on him as if your life depended on it – because it does. Use the power and authority of God to uproot, pull down, destroy and throw down.

- *Hammer Down* – Walls, barricades, barriers, hindrances, and blockages must be hammered down (*Jeremiah 23:29 Is not my word like as a fire? saith the LORD; and like a hammer that breaketh the rock in pieces?*) Sometimes these fortifications are made by us, sometimes the words and ideologies of others cause these walls and barriers, and sometimes they are made by the devil. Either way they need to come down. Use the hammer of God to break down walls and barriers that have been erected to hinder your breakthrough.

- *Run Through Troops* – Blast through groups of troops that keep you bound or that may be blocking your breakthrough (*Psalm 18:30 For by thee I have run through a troop; and by my God have I leaped over a wall*). If you read *Psalm 18:30-51*, you will discern that it is the power of God that enables you to do this. When you find yourself in tough life situations, ganged up on by demons or you come up against a stronghold that does not want to budge in your life, ask God to empower you to run through troops. Then as you pray and deal with these situations in your natural life, use your faith, power and authority to blast through these bondages.

- **Resist the Devil** – Stand against, oppose, withstand, set against the devil and all that concerns him (*James 4:7 Submit yourselves therefore to God. Resist the devil, and he will flee from you*). Before demons and filth will leave you, you have to fall out of agreement with it. The devil and his filth cannot stay if there is nothing in you wanting him to remain. You must break every covenant with it, divorce it, hate it, dread it being in you, and resist it from being a part of your life. Spend time breaking covenants with the devil, sin, pleasures of sin, mindsets, errors, and anything that keeps you in relationship with the enemy and his filthiness.

- **Breaking Soulties** – Soulties can be Godly or ungodly in nature. Just how generational curses are passed down, soulties are transferred from you and the other person and vice versa. Soulties can be formed through close friendships and interactions, covenants, vows, commitments, promises, physical intimacy, and etc. You can also have a soultie by having an unhealthy attachment to something or someone that has taken the place of God in your life or that has become an addiction in your life. Your soul, heart, mind, and body can be intertwined, bound, knitted, or in covenant with that person, place or thing. In addition, you exchange parts of yourself with the person you are in a soultie with. Parts of their personality, soul, heart, thoughts, mindsets, character, nature, and other deposits infuse you and begin to influence and live in you and vice versa. Also, whomever they have had relationship with and have not cleansed themselves of, is being passed on to you and vice versa.

- **Godly Soultie** – Soulties can be Godly and healthy. They possess the fruit and nature of God and empower your life, ministry, purpose and destiny. A healthy soultie has God's character, nature, fruit, will, and plan for our lives. As we can be tied to good things, but they may not necessarily be God's design.

    - ***1Samuel 18:1** And it came to pass, when he had made an end of speaking unto Saul, that the soul of Jonathan was knit with the soul of David, and Jonathan loved him as his own soul.*
    - ***Ecclesiastes 4:9-12 The Amplified Bible** Two are better than one, because they have a good [more satisfying] reward for their labor; For if they fall, the one will lift up his fellow. But woe to him who is alone when he falls and has not another to lift him up! Again, if two lie down together, then they have warmth; but how can one be warm alone? And though a man might prevail against him who is alone, two will withstand him. A threefold cord is not quickly broken.*
    - ***Matthew 18:19** Again I say unto you, That if two of you shall agree on earth as touching anything that they shall ask, it shall be done for them of my Father which is in heaven.*

- *Marriage Soultie* – When we get married, our lives are knitted in covenant with our spouse and we become one with them. There is no longer I, or two people. The two become one when married. You are of your spouse and your spouse is of you.
    - *Genesis 2:24 Therefore shall a man leave his father and his mother, and shall cleave unto his wife: and they shall be one flesh.*
    - *Matthew 19:5 And said, For this cause shall a man leave father and mother, and shall cleave to his wife: and they twain shall be one flesh?*

- *Ungodly Soultie* – An ungodly soultie is any knitting of ourselves with a person, place, or thing that is not of God or that is not God's will and plan for our lives. God will not have you bound to sin, idolatry, unhealthiness, unfruitfulness, or bondage. He will not have you engage or remain in a relationship that is a transgression against his word, will and plan for your life. God will not have you tie to something that is going to deplete you rather than build you in him and in your identity, purpose and destiny.
    - *Corinthians 6:16 What? know ye not that he which is joined to an harlot is one body? For two, saith he, shall be one flesh.*
    - *Genesis 34:1-3 And Dinah the daughter of Leah, which she bare unto Jacob went out to seethe daughters of the land. And when Shechem the son of Hamor the Hivite, prince of the country, saw her, he took her, and lay with her, and defiled her. And his soul clave unto Dinah the daughter of Jacob, and he loved the damsel, and spake kindly unto the damsel. Verse 8 And Hamor communed with them, saying the soul of my son Shechem longeth for your daughter: I pray you give her him to wife. Sexual involvement can form such entangling tentacles of soul ties that it is extremely hard to break off the relationship.*
    - *Proverbs 5:20-24 And why wilt thou, my son, be ravished with a strange woman, and embrace the bosom of a stranger? For the ways of man are before the eyes of the Lord, and he pondereth all his goings. His own iniquities shall take the wicked himself, and he shall be holden with the cords of his sins. He shall die without instruction; and in the greatness of his folly he shall go astray.*
    - *Psalms 1:1 Blessed is the man that walketh not in the counsel of the ungodly, nor standeth in the way of sinners, nor sitteth in the seat of the scornful*
    - *2Corinthians 6:14-18 Be ye not unequally yoked together with unbelievers: for what fellowship hath righteousness with unrighteousness? and what communion hath light with darkness? And what concord hath Christ with Belial? or what part hath he that believeth with an infidel? And what agreement hath the temple of God with idols? for ye are the temple of the living God; as God hath said, I will dwell in them, and walk in them; and I will be their God, and they shall be my people. Wherefore come out from among them, and be ye separate, saith the Lord, and touch not the unclean thing; and I will receive you, and will be a Father unto you, and ye shall be my sons and daughters, saith the Lord Almighty.*

- *Soultie with a Place* – You can be tied to a place and it can become a high place in your life, where you do not want to leave it or cannot leave it. You can be tied to a place where God has brought you out, but the tie keeps pulling you back in. Spiritually you are free, but your soul is bound to it. Lot's wife had a soultie with Sodom and Gomorrah. God was destroying the city because of the perversion, idolatry, lewdness, and lawlessness. God only allowed so many to live and allowed them time to get out of the city before he destroyed it. As they were walking out, Lot's wife looked back and turned into a pillar of salt.

    > *Genesis 19:23-26* *Then the Lord rained upon Sodom and upon Gomorrah brimstone and fire from the Lord out of heaven; And he overthrew those cities, and all the plain, and all the inhabitants of the cities, and that which grew upon the ground. But his wife looked back from behind him, and she became a pillar of salt.*

Even though God had graced Lot's wife with deliverance, her eyes and heart had regard for what she was leaving behind. Because her soul was still knitted to Sodom and Gomorrah, God caused her to perish with it. Being tied to something that God is freeing you from will deplete your life and even bring destruction upon you.

Agreement with God's will for the relationship along with healthiness is important in a Godly Soultie.

Amos 3:3 *Can two walk together, except they be agreed?*

The Message Bible *Do two people walk hand in hand if they aren't going to the same place?*

When the agreement is unhealthy, it makes for an ungodly soultie. Regardless of whether you agree or not, if a soultie is formed, it has to be broken in order for you to be free of whatever was knitted and transferred through that tie. This is vital, as rape, incest, abuse, mind control, religious sects, erred beliefs, etc. are ties that form without our agreement, out of ignorance, fear, or lack of knowledge, depending on the circumstance. When they are not broken, whatever the offender deposited lives in us. Some people result in manifesting traits of their offender, while others live in the false identity of what was deposited. Also, when you get divorced, it is best to break soulties with your ex-spouse. Many people have a difficult time moving forward because their souls are still tied to their ex-spouse. The covenant of marriage must be repented for and broken in the spirit realm, and soulties must be cleansed and broken so you can be free from all that was deposited and shared while married. It is important to break and cleanse soulties. This can be done by:

- Spending time before the Lord identifying every ungodly soultie you have in your life.
- Confessing and repenting for your role in the soultie, even if it was just giving into the lies and false identity of your offender.
- Forgiving the person you had a soultie with, and forgiving yourself for engaging in the soultie.

- Breaking and removing the soultie. Be sure to call out every person's name you have a soul tie with; go through these steps, and break and remove each tie.
- Using the blood of Jesus and the fire of God, cleanse yourself of all ungodly deposits, and command any parts of your soul, heart, mind and identity to be restored back to you.
- Occasionally spend time cleansing out any unhealthiness in your Godly soultie relationships, and any deposits that may have come from misunderstanding, miscommunication, taking one another for granted, being more to one another than God was saying, or becoming lax, fleshy or imbalanced in your interactions.

What did you learn as you read this chapter?

___

How beneficial will these cleansing tools be in helping you to maintain deliverance and healing regarding destiny and the entrepreneurial vision?

___

What negative attributes do you need to cleanse out of your destiny and entrepreneurial vision? Which cleansing tools will be sufficient in helping you to obtain breakthrough?

_____
_____
_____
_____
_____
_____
_____
_____
_____
_____
_____
_____
_____

BALANCING LIFE, DESTINY & THE VISION

Balance and self-care is essential to being healthy as you journey in destiny and as a vision carrier. Many people have trouble taking time to refresh. We tend to have a mindset that if we take time away:

- Things will not get done.
- People and duties will become stagnant or even regress.
- People and duties cannot survive and grow without us.
- We are failing or neglecting people or duties.
- We are failing God and our calling.
- We are failing the vision of our business, organization or ministry.
- We are not equipped as if we were we would not need respite.
- We are weak, as resting means we cannot handle what has been granted to our hands.

Most of our mindsets regarding resting is rooted in pride, as the focus is more about us and how our identity and self-worth is rooted in what we do, rather than who God is and what he does through us. Such a disposition is error as we constantly need to do and help in order to have a sense of value or self-importance. This is idolatry, because much of what we are doing is about building up our own kingdom, where we are glorified, rather than establishing God's kingdom where he is glorified. There is also a fear that someone will take what we have built, and even with blatant moral discrepancies, some feel they are above taking a sabbatical to be restored in God. This is pride at work as the focus is self. There is a false sense of security, and obligation in and to God, when really the person's trust and commitment is rooted in self, and in his or her accomplishments. This is a dangerous place to be in because the person operates as if God is with them, when really they have left the governing of God, and are now positioned for a great fall.

> *Proverbs 16:18* *Pride goeth before destruction, and a haughty spirit before a fall.*

It is important to note that you will need rest and the vision will require seasons of rest. When we feel the need to steal away with God, and when God tells us to rest, he is preparing us for a greater purpose than what is currently going on around us. The enemy and people do not enter a place of rest just because we desire to, or are unctioned to by the Lord. The enemy continues to be his same old devouring self, and people continue onward with their lives and issues. During times of rest, we notice the enemy's workings and the needs of the people all the more, because our defenses are down due to a posture of rest. We are also on the outside looking in, so we are seeing what is occurring and as caregivers, our life's purpose is to step in and save the day. However, when we continue to focus on the enemy and people's issues, rather than resting and seeking a refreshing in God, we are being disobedient, and we are uncovered from the protection of God. This gives the enemy a legal right to attack us, and people the right to weary and drain what little strength we have. We must be postured in a place of knowing that as we are obedient to God, he will fortify us from the lurking enemy, and take care of the people we are to help.

One of the Greek words for *rest* is *anapausis* and means:
1. intermission; by implication, recreation, rest
2. cessation of any motion, business or labour

Rest is a literal putting to death of your works. The only way to enter true rest is to cease all works, and not be drawn into battles that are not God ordained.

> *Matthew 11:28-30 Come unto me, all ye that labour and are heavy laden, and I will give you rest. Take my yoke upon you, and learn of me; for I am meek and lowly in heart: and ye shall find rest unto your souls. For my yoke is easy, and my burden is light.*

Moreover, there is a changing of guards in the place of rest. You exchange your strength and workings for God's easy yoke and burden.

God promises refuge and lightheartedness when there is a true positioning of rest. At times, we are not able to discern the refuge because resting usually manifests what is already unrested/disquieted within us. If we are anxious, agitated, murmuring, complaining, sick, tired of warring, overworked, over-burdened, etc., it is usually an indication of the weariness that is already in us, and is the reason God required a time of rest in the first place.

We tend to see such irritations as being from the enemy and the enemy harassing us in our rest, but this is not the enemy, this is what needs to be cleansed out of us - exchanging our overburdened soul for a refreshing of our soul. We simply recognize these things now because we do not have people, the enemy, trials, war, duties and labor to distract us. If we really enter a place of rest, these harassments manifesting from within us will dissolve, and then the enemy will not have a foothold in our time of rest to heighten, and take advantage of these open doors in our lives.

Rest is a fixed and stable place or position. In this place, the leader is not wandering in and out of rest. The leader is submitted to being seated in God, and their work is centered on staying grounded and postured in this position.

> *Psalms 91:1-2 The Amplified Bible HE WHO dwells in the secret place of the Most High shall remain stable and fixed under the shadow of the Almighty [Whose power no foe can withstand]. I will say of the Lord, He is my Refuge and my Fortress, my God; on Him I lean and rely, and in Him I [confidently] trust!*

> *The Message Bible You who sit down in the High God's presence, spend the night in Shaddai's shadow, Say this: God, you're my refuge. I trust in you and I'm safe!*

> *Hebrews 4:11 Let us labour therefore to enter into that rest, lest any man fall after the same example of unbelief.*

The Amplified Bible *Let us therefore be zealous and exert ourselves and strive diligently to enter that rest [of God, to know and experience it for ourselves], that no one may fall or perish by the same kind of unbelief and disobedience [into which those in the wilderness fell].*

As we further consider ***Mathew 11:28***,

<u>Labour is *spoudazo* in the Greek and means:</u>
1. seed (used in sowing): to use speed, i. e. to make effort, be prompt or earnest, do
2. (give) diligence, be diligent (forward), endeavor, labour, study
3. due diligence, be diligent, give diligence, be forward, labour, study
4. to hasten, make haste, to exert one's self

The Greek word for labor denotes that when we are diligent to enter a place of rest in God, it is seed used for sowing. We sow into being diligent to rest and God rewards us by doing or leading us in doing all the work that needs to be done in us and for us. We are totally submitted to His strength and His spirit, and do nothing of and in our own accord.

It is therefore, important to have a passion in staying in this place when God is requiring it of you. Pursue it with passion like you would pursue anything that you deem important and be okay with ceasing from works, personal pulls and pulls of people, or obligations and responsibilities that will only drain you and steal your time of renewal in God.

<u>Another Greek words for *rest* is *katapausis* and means:</u>
1. reposing down, i. e. (by Hebraism) abode
2. a putting to rest calming of the winds, a resting place
3. metaph. the heavenly blessedness in which God dwells, and of which he has promised to make persevering believers in Christ partakers after the toils and trials of life on earth are ended

<u>Dictionary.com defines *repose* as:</u>
1. to lie at rest
2. to lie dead
3. to remain still or concealed
4. to take a rest
5. to rest for support: lie

As we are diligent in pursuing such a place of rest and calmness, our spiritual and natural posture should literally appear as dead. Also, unhealthy things should die in us just because we have been obedient to resting in God.

Repose suggests that this rest should be as a death. The quietness we enter should be in such submission that we appear dead from doing works. We should be totally submitted and focused on being humbled, bowed and prostrate before Jesus.

> *Hebrews 4::12 New Living Bible says: For the word of God is living and active and sharper than any double- edged sword, piercing even to the point of dividing soul from spirit, and joints from marrow; it is able to judge the desires and thoughts of the heart. And no creature is hidden from God, a but everything is naked and exposed to the eyes of him to whom we must render an account.*

This asserts that we are not trying to hide our sins, faults, or weariness, but are taking them to him - before him. As we are diligent in resting, his word goes in and surgically removes everything that is not like him. It divides the good from the bad and cleanses us (our souls), then renews and reconnects us (our spirits) in places that were disconnected from him.

> ***The Message Bible*** *God means what he says. What he says goes. His powerful Word is sharp as a surgeon's scalpel, cutting through everything, whether doubt or defense, laying us open to listen and obey. Nothing and no one is impervious to God's Word. We can't get away from it--no matter what.*

> ***The Amplified Bible*** *Let us therefore be zealous and exert ourselves and strive diligently to enter that rest [of God, to know and experience it for ourselves], that no one may fall or perish by the same kind of unbelief and disobedience [into which those in the wilderness fell]. For the Word that God speaks is alive and full of power [making it active, operative, energizing, and effective]; it is sharper than any two- edged sword, penetrating to the dividing line of the breath of life (soul) and [the immortal] spirit, and of joints and marrow [of the deepest parts of our nature], exposing and sifting and analyzing and judging the very thoughts and purposes of the heart.*

<u>Sharper</u> is <u>tomoteros</u> <u>in the Greek and means:</u>
1. to cut; more comprehensive or decisive than, as if by a single stroke
2. whereas that implies repeated blows, like hacking
3. more keen, sharper

What did you learn from this chapter?

_____
_____
_____
_____
_____
_____
_____
_____
_____
_____

What reasons do you think I added this chapter to this book? What reasons is rest essential to your destiny and effectiveness as a vision carrier?

_____
_____
_____
_____
_____
_____
_____
_____
_____
_____
_____
_____
_____
_____
_____
_____
_____
_____
_____
_____

What challenges if any do you have with resting and taking breaks?

_____
_____
_____
_____
_____
_____
_____
_____
_____
_____

List three goals you can work on to improve your taking time to refresh and truly resting inside the presence of the Lord.

_____
_____
_____
_____
_____
_____
_____
_____
_____
_____
_____
_____
_____
_____
_____
_____
_____
_____

SUGGESTIONS FOR TAKING RESPITE

In addition to daily prayer and study, you should be taking weekly time to just replenish before the Lord, and just for leisure purposes. Jesus encouraged the disciples in this area:

Mark 6:30-32 reads: And he said unto them, Come ye yourselves apart into a desert place, and rest a while: for there were many coming and going, and they had no leisure so much as to eat.

These wisdom keys can be implemented for short and long-term times of respite.

- Decide how much time you are going to take and stick to your regimen (e.g. A few hours, one day, three days, seven days, twenty-one days, forty days).

- If it is for a few hours, give yourself that time without feeling like you have to share it with anyone. Just take it. God knows what can occur during that time and if something happens that you need to be a part of, he will unction you. Moses was experiencing the weighty glory and instruction of the Lord and God said to him "*Go, get thee down; for thy people, which thou broughtest out of the land of Egypt, have corrupted themselves*" (*Exodus 32:7*). If you are needed, God will make sure you know.

- Establish a day just for you during the week so people will know you are off limits for that day. If your respite is for a longer period of time, let those close to you know that you will not be available for those amount of days, and to only contact you in case of emergency. If you have a ministry, let those who you oversee know you will not be available, and put someone in charge that can oversee the ministry while you are resting.

- If you are married and have children, tell your spouse of your respite plans and ask him or her to come into agreement with giving you this time of refreshing. Let the children know as well, and have them go to your spouse for whatever they need. Depending on your home environment, you may have to take respite outside of the home. Be okay with doing this. You cannot adequately be there for your family if you have nothing to give. Your family can also leave the home and give you time at home with Jesus. Some leaders have time during the day for respite, while everyone is away. It is important to schedule that time in a few days a week, where it is just you and Jesus. Be disciplined in your other duties and responsibilities, while making this a balanced priority in your life.

- Log off of all social media and messenger sites. These are an asset not a priority. If you have built a ministry through these sites, and they are rooted in the Lord, then they will keep. You do not have to operate in fear where you are deceived into believing that if you do not feed people every day, they will not follow you. They should not be drawn to you, but to the God in you. This is another avenue the enemy is draining people and leaders, and they do not recognize it. Many social media people are fickle and flighty. They feed on the next catchy word or trend, but rarely are they implementing what is spoken in their lives to produce real change. Jesus is not about tickling people's fancies. He is about saving and transforming lives. Be focused on transforming people rather than gorging them with revelation that their lives and spiritual walks cannot digest. Delete the apps off your devices if you have to. Do whatever you need to do to close in with Jesus.

- If your rest time is longer than three days then commit to checking emails, texts, and phone call messages once a day. Only respond to what is important and immediately requires attention. Put a 30-minute time limit on this so that you are not being drawn back into works when you should be resting. Unless it is a life or death situation, delegate any other emergency and duties to a responsible party, and return to communion with the Lord. And even with life and death situations, you must recognize that all things are in God's hands. Jesus was about his father's business when Lazarus died, and some of it included him resting and refreshing before the Lord. Jesus was challenged by Lazarus' death, how others responded to Lazarus' death, had compassion for their grief, and he also was grieved to the point of weeping. However, Jesus did not feel guilty because Lazarus died, nor did he take on the guilt others tried to put upon him. He also raised Lazarus from the dead. You have the power to resurrect anything that dies once you return from your time of rest and being about your father's business of getting what you need from him, so you can walk in pure power and authority (**Read John 11:32-45**).

- This time of rest is for you. You are not praying for anyone else, praying for the ministry, interceding, etc., unless God leads you to do so. Otherwise, it is time for you to take yourself before God, so he can replenish and renew you.

- You may have to spend the first few minutes, hours, or days of your rest time releasing people and duties to JESUS and breaking soulties to them. *Matthew 11:28-30 says Come unto me, all ye that labour and are heavy laden, and I will give you rest. Take my yoke upon you, and learn of me; for I am meek and lowly in heart: and ye shall find rest unto your souls. For my yoke is easy, and my burden is light.* You will have to release the yoke of people, ministry, and life, and anyway you are tied and obligated to them and take on the yoke of the Lord. You will know there is an unhealthy yoke when you are trying to pray for yourself and press into Jesus, but that person, situation, concern, or duty keeps coming into your mind/heart, and drawing your attention away from you and God. Break ties with it, and surrender it to the greatest hands it could be in which is Jesus. If this does not work, then search if it belongs in this time of prayer with you and Jesus. If Jesus says it does, then allow Jesus to direct you in how to pray, journal, or approach it.

- As you surrender matters to God, pursue God, repent for sin issues and character flaws, etc., and also take time to receive. So often we are talking and pressing in through a hunger and desire for a great encounter with God, until we do not realize God is with us, and is pouring himself into us. Take time in silence while just resting in the presence of the Lord. Just wait in the Lord. If he talks that is okay. If he does not talk, that is okay too. He is your friend. You do not talk to your friend the entire time you are hanging out. Sometimes you are quiet and just resting and being together. Be okay with doing this with the Lord. You do not have to gimmick and perform for God, and please do not require him to gimmick and perform for you. Wait in courage that he is with you and is enjoying rest time with you. *Psalms 27:14 Wait on the Lord: be of good courage, and he shall strengthen thine heart: wait, I say, on the Lord.*

- Be okay with falling asleep. Some of you need to sleep. Sleep is spiritual, healthy, and brings healing and direction. *Psalms 63:6 When I remember thee upon my bed, and meditate on thee in the night watches. Psalms 4:4 Stand in awe, and sin not: commune with your own heart upon your bed, and be still. Selah. Psalms 16:7 I will bless the LORD, who hath given me counsel: my reins also instruct me in the night seasons. Isaiah 26:11 With my soul have I desired thee in the night; yea, with my spirit within me will I seek thee early: for when thy judgments are in the earth, the inhabitants of the world will learn righteousness.* At the moment you SHIFT into personal rest, you are deciding to enter a night season. You have blacked the rest of the world out and you are in a time of communion with the Lord. The only light you should be seeing is his glory light. God releases dreams, visions, instructions, and strategies while we sleep. I often hear God talking to me in my sleep. He will have me get up and journal things he shares and then I will return to sleep where I am communing with him. *Proverbs 3:24 When thou liest down, thou shalt not be afraid: yea, thou shalt lie down, and thy sleep shall be sweet.* When something is sweet it is pleasant, delightful, refreshing, enjoyable, joyful. This is one-way God cleanses heaviness, depression, stress, and frustration. He does it with good sleep. Sometimes you can feel the Holy Spirit healing and refreshing you as you sleep. Sometimes you are just experiencing good sound sleep. If you get sleepy, go to sleep and trust that because you took time with God, he knows what you have need of. *Psalms 3:5 I lay down and slept; I awoke, for the LORD sustains me.*

- Sometimes we lie down in prayer with God and we are so engulfed in his presence that we go into a trancelike state where we feel like we cannot move. We feel like we are in between being sleep and awake. Be okay when experiencing this. God does some of his best healing and communing in this state. He is satiating and replenishing you. Satiate means "*to bathe, to satisfy, to soak, and to fill you up.*" *Jeremiah 31:25-26 For I have satiated the weary soul, and I have replenished every sorrowful soul. Upon this I awaked, and beheld; and my sleep was sweet unto me.* **The Amplified Bible** *For I will [fully] satisfy the weary soul, and I will replenish every languishing and sorrowful person. Thereupon I [Jeremiah] awoke and looked, and my [trancelike] sleep was sweet [in the assurance it gave] to me.*

- Have a journal, pin, and bible handy so you can scribe whatever God shares and study scripture as God leads. A recorder can also be beneficial if you want to record any words of prophecy, knowledge, strategy, and counsel that the Lord gives. These words will still need to be written so the vision can be engraved (imparted and established) into the earth realm, where you and others can read and utilize it. *Isaiah 30:8 Now go, write it before them in a table, and note it in a man, that it may be for the time to come for ever and ever.* **Habakkuk 2:2** *And the LORD answered me, and said, Write the vision, and make it plain upon tables, that he may run that readeth it.*

Example Of A Personal Wellness Vision Plan

Block these times out on your calendar so you will not give this time away to anything else, and so you can be accountable to your personal wellness plan.

- Take a personal leisure day every Monday.
- Pray at 5am to 7am Tuesday - Friday (An hour of that is just you and Jesus and the other is for people and ministry).
- Saturday is flexible and Sunday, and Monday pray 7am to 9am (An hour of that is just you and Jesus and the other is for people and ministry).
- Fast Tuesdays and Thursdays until 6pm water only.
- Work on sermons and teachings 12pm to 2pm on Tuesdays and Thursdays
- Exercise Wednesday, Thursday, Friday at 9am for 45 minutes.
- Counseling and mentoring hours Wednesday and Saturday from 9am to 12pm and from 2pm to 5pm.
- Take a quarterly three day personal fast and consecration sabbatical where it is just time with God (March, June, September).
- Take a sabbatical the second week of November to the first week of January of the next year.

Use the suggestions and examples above to write your own personal plan for wellness and respite. Share your plan with your tribe so they can keep you accountable to maintaining self-care.

BALANCING FAMILY & RELATIONSHIPS

Balancing Dating & Engaged Relationships:

- If you are dating or engaged, be honest about your ministry schedule and your times of prayer and study with the Lord. Role model your schedule, rather than giving the impression that you have free time that you do not really have. Let the person know the reason God has required the specific disciplines for you so they can pray concerning what you are sharing, and have a clear vision of who you are in God.

- Seek the Lord together for any changes you each need to make in each of your spiritual walks to make time for one another.

- Create a vision plan for cultivating your relationship and commit to working it.

- Schedule prayer and study time together. This will help with your transition if you have been single for a while, and are used to spending a lot of time praying, studying and doing ministry. This will also help you build one another up in the Lord.

- Have a balance between attending ministering activities and leisure time. Be cognizant of not just spending time together at ministry events. Schedule leisure events that you both may enjoy, but do not hinder or jeopardize your walk with the Lord.

- Communicate when you feel neglected or torn between the relationship and ministry. Encourage the other person to do the same. Commit to not holding back your thoughts and feelings in this area as it will cause an open door to division and strife. Communication is key to giving your thoughts and feelings a voice in the relationship, and to getting your needs and desires met. You must be able to communicate, because the Lord will not tell you every single thing no matter how anointed you are. This will cause you to grow in being honest and vulnerable with one another in your desires, needs, and standards.

- If you are dating or engaged, the Lord will give you grace to sustain the relationship. In busy seasons, time will be stretched. You must set aside special time for one another knowing God has given you the grace to walk in the relationship. He released the relationship in due time knowing you could balance ministry, work life, and personal relationship. Therefore, be okay with working through these seasons.

- Be able to celebrate one another. You are not in competition with one another but there to support, strengthen, and esteem each other greater than yourselves as you move forward in unity. No one wants to date or become engaged with someone who cannot genuinely celebrate their success. You must be willing to gut out any subtle jealousy, inadequacy, or revenge of wanting to perform better than your potential spouse.

- Please know that whatever you root in your foundation will be difficult to gut out in the future. It is important to have a balanced healthy foundation that your relationship can stand on.

Balancing Marriage and Family Relationships:

- Make weekly time for your marriage and family. Schedule it on your calendar and make it a priority. Ensure you schedule time for just your spouse alone, as well as the entire family. Remember to never stop dating your spouse! It is also important to confirm on a regular frequency that the scheduled time is a time that works for the family and change it as needed, but do all you can to not cancel it.

- Resist adding events to your calendar that are not a part of what God is requiring of you in the present season you are in. Make sure you communicate and share your calendar with your spouse and family, to ensure that their needs are covered during these times and/or adjustments can be made.

- Resist enabling people and having meetings where people just want to waste time, but are not about true change.

- Trust your team and promote accountability. If they cannot be accountable then replace them with someone who can. A lot of times, we keep people in positions to avoid conflict, but this is at the expense of you having to step in and do it. Replace them with someone that can be accountable, so you do not have to spend your time fulfilling duties that others can do.

- Pace yourself in your ministry vision. Be cognizant to hearing God concerning what you need to be working on at any given season, so you will not stretch yourself too thin.

- Be disciplined in scheduling meetings and completing ministry duties when other family members are busy so you all can be working at the same time, as opposed to hitting and missing one another. If there is a time that this cannot be accomplished, it is important that you communicate this to your family and be disciplined with the scheduled time.

- Invite and implement your family into your ministry endeavors and what God is doing in your life. Often we are selfish and protective in this area without realizing that it can cause family members to be jealous of your relationship with God and your ministry. It can also cause wounds and conflicts where there are demands to choose between the two. Ask your family for feedback on your ministry endeavors and be open to hearing them. This will help them feel a part of this portion of your life verses separating the two. Remember your family is your primary ministry!

- Every marriage and family are different. It is okay to consider suggestions from others, but it is best to search God for a vision plan for your marriage and family. What works for others may not work for your marriage and family. Consult with your spouse and family concerning the plan, and give them the opportunity to change and add to the plan. The vision plan can include how you desire your relationships to be, desires of spending time together, commitments to supporting one another's life events, activities and outings you all can plan and do together, and etc. Revisit the plan every few months to make sure it still works for your current family dynamics and adjust it accordingly.

- Do not try to fit ministry duties and obligations that may arise in particular seasons, inside the dynamics of your marriage and family. Take time to evaluate what season you are in with God, and share what God has said with your spouse and family. Then together you all explore with God, what standards will be needed to complete the will of God, while also remaining committed to the family needs and desires.

- Text, call, and email to express affirmations of love, appreciation, support, and encouragement. Ensure that you are communicating in a fashion that fits each family members' needs. While your child may receive from a text message, your spouse may prefer a call, so they can hear your voice. Know what each family member needs and desires, and engage them accordingly. Also, make sure they are aware of your needs and desires, so they can bring fulfillment to your life.

- Consistently check on your spouse and families' well-being. Show concern for their soul with such fervor as you would those under your ministry. At no point should your family feel as if they lack priority in your life.

- Plan family vacations that are not centered around ministry. It is important that you spend time connecting and making memories with your family to ensure continued balance for both you and your family. It can be as simple as a weekend trip, or a 7-day trip. The key is you are making time to focus on them. Consider and plan separate trips for just you and your spouse, and then one with the entire family at least once a year.

- Speak into your family and make sure their spiritual needs are met. They need to see and know that you care about their spiritual growth just as much and more than those you are assigned to in the Kingdom.

What areas do you need to improve in relations to balancing marriage, children, family, dating, and friendships?

_____
_____
_____
_____

What are the biggest challenges you have with taking personal time to be with family and friends?

Use the suggestions above to write a vision plan that you and your family can realistically implement into your daily lives.

ESTABLISHING SUCCESSORS

God is all about generational inheritance. One of the challenges with many ministries, businesses, organizations, and cultures is they do not seriously consider those that should be inheriting what they plant in the earth, or how to establish a vision, and mentor others, so that the vision can be passed down and maintained throughout the generations. All through the bible we see how mighty men blessed their children, and put them in charge of keeping the lineage fertile and productive. We see this with Jacob and Essau, David and Solomon, Elijah and Elisha, Paul and Timothy, Jesus and the Disciples, and on and on.

Some people fear grooming a successor. This fear is often understandable in some instances, as at times there can be those who have impure motives regarding being a part of your entrepreneurial vision. However, seeking God for revelation of your successor is vital to making sure you choose the right person, and that that person/s has God's heart and mandate to successfully GOVERN and CARRY your vision. As you consider successors, examine the following questions before the Lord.

What is the longevity of your vision, book, etc.? Is it seasonal or eternal?

_____
_____
_____
_____
_____
_____
_____
_____
_____
_____
_____

What does the successor of your vision, book, etc. look like? (This is important in making sure what you plant sustains throughout the generations).

- Are they a biological child, spiritual child, mentee, helper in the vision?
- Do you have more than one successor? What portions of the vision do you see them carrying?
- What are their character traits? How is their character and integrity?
- Are they teachable? Are they life learners?
- Do they have a relationship with God? Are they sold out to God?
- What do they need to work on to take over your vision and sustain it? (**Luke 14:27-28** *And whosoever doth not bear his cross, and come after me, cannot be my disciple. For which of you, intending to build a tower, sitteth not down first, and counteth the cost*).
- Do they have a heart for you and for the vision? Do they honor you and the vision?

- What is their work ethic?
- Are they invested in the vision and seeing it flourishing in the earth?
- Do they help you to produce the vision in the earth (they may walk with you in seasons and assist or they may be a vision carrier)?
- What are their giftings and calling – life's purpose?
- How does their giftings, calling, impact, benefit, grow your vision?
- How can you empower them in their giftings and callings and enable them to establish their vision in the earth?
- How can you empower them to be able to sustain in their vision and in the successorship they will receive through your vision?
- Do they have a heart for the region and spheres of influence God has called you to? Is the vision mobile or able to be established in different regions if necessary? Are they able to do the work to replant or expand your vision in a different region or sphere of influence?
- Ask God for a time frame to discuss them being successors and for grooming them as successors. Know that you will have to mentor them so that they are able to carry your vision and even pass it down to the next and the next and the next generation, until Jesus returns.

As you are working your vision, make sure you are building a foundation that your successor can build upon. Journal some thoughts of what they may look like.

_____
_____
_____
_____
_____
_____
_____
_____
_____
_____
_____
_____
_____

Leave blue prints and even this book and other documents for them to follow. If you know who they are, train them as you are planting and working the vision, so they will have clarity of the vision, value of the work ethic needed to sustain the vision, can be groomed in the character and nature of God to honor God, the vision, and the honor needed for the vision to be sustained in the earth.

    Proverbs 16:3 *Commit your work to the Lord, and your plans will be established.*

    Psalms 115:14 *The Lord shall increase you more and more, you and your children.*

    Proverbs 13:22 *A good man leaveth an inheritance to his children's children: and the wealth of the sinner is laid up for the just.*

    Psalms 145:4 *One generation shall commend your works to another, and shall declare your mighty acts.*

    Genesis *28:18 And in your offspring shall all the nations of the earth be blessed, because you have obeyed my voice."*

What revelation did you receive as you meditated on these scriptures?

_____
_____
_____
_____
_____

YEAR END REFLECTION & NEW YEAR GOALS

EVERY YEAR AROUND NOVEMBER, I use this plan as a time of reflection of the previous year and exploration of the coming year. I also give this plan to my leadership team, close spiritual children and mentees that I do life with. I give them a month to complete it, and I individually meet with each of them and share successes, constructive criticism, direction and prophecies God has given me concerning them for the upcoming year.

A year end plan is essential to:

- Keeping you accountable to fulfilling goals and prophecies
- Remaining in the momentum of God as a vision carrier
- Making sure you achieve goals and prophecies
- Assessing your progress and achievements, and taking time to celebrate the successes of your journey
- Assessing what may have occurred that caused you not to achieve goals and prophecies
- Assessing whether goals and prophecies need to be added to next year's plan or taken off the plan altogether
- Assessing whether God desires new goals and different strategies to further work the vision in the coming year
- Seeking God for strategies and prophecies to successfully carry the vision in the upcoming year

Use the following questions to seek God regarding your year-end plan

1. *What has your spiritual progress and challenges been like this year?*

2. *What has been the most enjoyable times of this year? Explain your answer in detail. Spend time thanking God for these moments.*

   _____
   _____
   _____
   _____
   _____
   _____
   _____
   _____
   _____
   _____
   _____
   _____
   _____
   _____
   _____
   _____
   _____
   _____
   _____

3. *What has been the most challenging times of this year? Explain your answer in detail. Spend time releasing challenges and asking God to deliver and heal you where necessary.*

   _____
   _____
   _____
   _____
   _____
   _____
   _____
   _____
   _____
   _____
   _____
   _____
   _____
   _____

4. Did you achieve your goals and what God desired of you personally, spiritually and as a vision carrier? Explain your progress or lack thereof in detail. What would you do differently? What would you do better? Explain in detail.

___

5. How did your ministry covering or those you are affiliated with impact your progress, growth and/or lack thereof this year?

___

6. What is God saying for you personally for the New Year?

7. *What is God saying for you regarding your entrepreneurial endeavors as it relates to the New Year?*

8. *What needs to be changed or added to your personal and entrepreneurial vision plan to help you maintain the standards and accountabilities needed to achieve your goals?*

9. *What is God saying to you as it relates to the ministry covering or those you are affiliated and walking with in this season? (e.g. How are they to impact this season, do you need to seek other partners or mentors, are their relationships or partnerships you need to end in this season that are not beneficial to the vision or no longer needed for the vision or for your destiny?)*

What disciplines do you need to achieve your personal goals?

10. *What disciplines do you need to achieve your entrepreneurial goals?*

11. *What do you desire and feel you need from your covering, mentors, or leaders to achieve your goals?*

12. What do you need from God to achieve your goals?

13. *List three goals you are committed to working on to achieve the things God is requiring of you.*

14. *List three goals you are committed to working on to grow in your gifts and callings where you can continually mature the mantle and anointing upon your life (e.g. read books, attend webinars, workshops, conferences, take courses, increase prayer and study life, be mentored by someone with a like vision or mantle, etc.)*

15. *Share anything else that would benefit what God is asking of you in the upcoming year (e.g. fears, worries, concerns, hesitancies, excitement, etc.) Spend time releasing challenges to the Lord and allowing him to empower you with courage and confidence, while giving you a strategy to further combat these challenges. Journal the strategies he gives and use them throughout the year to protect yourself, empower, and tower in your vision.*

_____
_____
_____
_____
_____
_____
_____
_____
_____
_____
_____
_____
_____
_____
_____
_____
_____
_____
_____
_____

16. *List five scriptures to help you ground your new year's vision in the principles of the word.*

_____
_____
_____
_____
_____
_____
_____
_____
_____
_____
_____
_____
_____
_____

VISIONARY CHARGE! SHIFT!

I charge you to live in a lifestyle of destiny with God.

I charge you to never be less than who God has created you to be.

I charge you to release your vision on earth, breathe eternal life in it through your worth ethic, and solidify a unique representation of you in the earth until Jesus comes.

I charge you to never give up.

I charge you to never compare yourself or covet someone else's destiny or life's vision.

I charge you to value and love who you are and what God has called you to do in the earth.

I charge you to be a good steward over your finances.

I charge you to remain humble, integral and rooted in Godly character at every level of success and destiny attainment.

I charge you to be fulfilled in your covenant with God as you journey with him in destiny.

I charge you to be a violent kingdom warrior over your destiny and life's vision.

I charge you to take the kingdom by force. SEIZE IT!

I charge you to never brag about warfare, but to tower over every devil no matter their rank.

I charge you to teach others to war and intercede over their destinies and entrepreneurial visions.

I charge you to be a generational curse breaker, and to restore the fullness of salvation in your family lineage.

I charge you to write the vision and make it plain in writing, in action, and with your lifestyle.

I charge you to never take short cuts and to never despise small beginnings or hard seasons. They will work for your good.

I charge you to be honest about your progress and process in every season of life, access your goals, repent when you fall short, and make changes to improve where necessary.

I charge you to be a lifelong learner, so you can always grow in destiny and in your entrepreneurial vision. For level to level and glory to glory shall you always SHIFT and triumph.

I charge you to freely give to others as you receive.

I charge you to raise up successors who can sustain your vision and even pass it on to other generations.

YOU CAN DO IT! I AM ALREADY PROUD OF YOU! SHIFT!

# KINGDOM SHIFTERS NETWORK

KSM is an apostolic network that has been called to raise up Kingdom Shifters in the earth and to assist them with journeying successfully in their God ordained destiny and entrepreneurial vision. This clarion call requires us to aide apostolic leadership to effectively build, pioneer, and father Kingdom Shifters so they can leave a legacy that generations can gleam from. By joining KSM, Kingdom Shifters become aligned, edified, and equipped to advance the kingdom of God.

If you need covering, partnership, and equipping in journeying in your destiny and entrepreneurial vision, please contact Taquetta Baker via email at kingdomshifters@gmail.com.

BOOK REFERENCES

- *Apostolic Mantle By Taquetta Baker*

- *Blueletterbible.com*

- *Biblestudytools.com*

- *Dictionary.com*

- *Healing The Wounded Leader Manual By Taquetta Baker*

- *Kingdom Decrees For Sustaining The Vision By Taquetta Baker*

- *Olivetree.com*

- *Spurned Into Apostleship By Jackie Green*

- *Strongs Exhaustive Bible Concordance Online Bible Study Tools*

- *Wikipedia*

- *Cover photo by Reenita Keys. Connect with her via Facebook.*

- *Editing by Amanda Latrice Connect with her via Facebook*

Kingdom Shifters Books & Apparel
Available at Kingdomshifters.com

BOOKS FOR EVERYONE

Healing The Wounded Leader	Feasting In His Presence
Kingdom Shifters Decree That Thang	Kingdom Heirs Decree That Thing
Kingdom Watchman Builder on the Wall	Let There Be Sight
Embodiment Of A Kingdom Watchman	Apostolic Governing Of Destiny
Dismantling Homosexuality Handbook	Annihilating the Powers of Church Hurt
Releasing The Vision	Atmosphere Changers (Weaponry
Apostolic Mantle	Sustaining The Vision

BOOKS FOR DANCE MINISTERS

Dancers! Dancers! Decree That Thang

Dance & The Fivefold

Spirits That Attack Dance Ministers & Ministries

Dance From Heaven To Earth

TEE SHIRTS

Kingdom Shifters Tee Shirt	Let The Fruit Speak Tee Shirt
Releasing The Vision Tee Shirt	Kingdom Perspective Tee Shirt
Stand in Position Tee Shirt	No Defense Tee Shirt
My God Rules Like A Boss Tee Shirt	Destiny Blueprint Tee Shirt

CD'S

Decree That Thing CD

Kingdom Heirs Decree That Thing CD